I, MARGARET

The Unauthorised Autobiography

as told to
STEVE NALLON
with
TOM HOLT

M

PAPERMAC

First published in 1989 by
PAPERMAC
a division of Macmillan Publishers Limited
4 Little Essex Street London WC2R 3LF
and Basingstoke

Associated companies in Auckland, Delhi, Dublin, Gaborone,
Hamburg, Harare, Hong Kong, Johannesburg, Kuala Lumpur,
Lagos, Manzini, Melbourne, Mexico City, Nairobi, New York,
Singapore and Tokyo

ISBN 0-333-49776-7

A CIP catalogue record for this book is available
from the British Library

Photoset by Rowland Phototypesetting Limited
Bury St Edmunds, Suffolk
Printed in Great Britain by
Billing & Sons Ltd, Worcester

Contents

PROLOGUE
A Woman's Work

[1]

CHAPTER ONE
A Child is Born

[9]

CHAPTER TWO
Seeds of Glory

[37]

CHAPTER THREE
Ninety Per Cent Perspiration

[53]

CHAPTER FOUR
A Mother's Joy

[73]

CHAPTER FIVE
My Burgeoning Destiny

[91]

CHAPTER SIX
By the Grace of God

[115]

CHAPTER SEVEN
Send Her Victorious

[131]

CHAPTER EIGHT
Rejoice, Rejoice

[143]

POSTSCRIPT
We are a Grandmother

[169]

ACKNOWLEDGEMENTS

[173]

INDEX

[175]

Dedicated to a grateful nation

PROLOGUE

A Woman's Work

Many people have said that the office of Prime Minister is fraught with difficulties. I have never found this. Perhaps the reason is that I was brought up to keep things neat and tidy, and as a result my office is orderly, properly dusted and, above all, immaculately clean. This is, of course, because I see to it myself.

Every day, before starting work, I take the time and trouble to run a duster over the desk and pick up any paperclips or treasury tags which may have fallen on the carpet. I strongly believe that waste and inefficiency in any form and on all levels is fatal to good housekeeping and, as every housewife knows, running the country is very much like running a house. So woe betide any member of the Downing Street staff who leaves a window grimy or a cushion unplumped!

In many ways, I like to think that my office is a reflection of myself. The walls are a discreet shade of pale cream and the curtains are good hard-wearing brocade. I always insist on one feminine touch; there is invariably a small vase of flowers on my desk, which my Private Secretary gathers in St James's Park every morning.

My day starts early, as it has always done. I rarely sleep more than a few hours at night, since I hold that sleep softens the brain. If I find it necessary to sleep, there are plenty of opportunities during the day – a speech by Sir Geoffrey Howe in the House, for example, or a policy briefing at the Ministry of Employment. As soon as I wake up in the morning I switch on the radio to see what has been happening while I have been unconscious. Generally I make a point of listening to Radio Four, despite the sadly left-wing bias of most of its current-affairs reporting. I have known socialists to be inter-viewed on the radio before nine o'clock in the morning. How irresponsible! Children might be listening. Never-theless there is no alternative; the last time I happened to twiddle the dial, I had the misfortune to come across Radio Two. Although I waited patiently for over five minutes there was no news bulletin; all I heard was a music programme, with a man called Andy Williams singing 'The Fool on the Hill' – a favourite song of mine, incidentally; I was once even moved to write a new lyric for it about Ted Heath, called 'The Fool over the Hill'.

After I have cooked Denis's breakfast – two slices of toast and dripping with a wholesome glass of cold water – and laid out suitable clothes for him to wear during the day, I am able to get down to some work. Of course I never read the newspapers, except for the *Daily Telegraph* and the more useful sections of the *Financial Times*, since they tend to consist of nothing but scurrilous libels by Communist agitators and malcontents. Fortunately, my Press Secretary is on hand to make a selection for me and after all vindictive personal attacks have been left out I am generally left with the Australian football results and some of the gardening tips, which I find most absorbing.

Occasionally too a 'human interest' story catches my eye, and I like to read these since they can sometimes give a valuable insight into what ordinary people are thinking. For example, I was most interested in 1989 by the reports of an outbreak of food poisoning in the House of Commons, when a virus called pamellabordes struck down several MPs and even affected the Press Gallery.

Denis and I live in the flat on the top floor of

10 Downing Street. Once it had become apparent that I was likely to be living there for the foreseeable future, I decided to redecorate it. Naturally, this was done at my own expense, using some free paint and wallpaper kindly supplied by one of our leading firms. As it turned out the gift was most timely, since the wallpaper we had removed from the walls of our old home at Flood Street turned out to be nearly a foot too short. Now that we have got Number Ten just as we like it, Denis no longer regrets leaving our former home in Flood Street. He has lately taken to practising long putts on the floor of the Cabinet Room when everyone has gone home, and his only complaint is that he finds all those flights of stairs up to our flat rather difficult when he returns in the early hours of the morning after a fraught board meeting.

There is nothing lavish or grand about our flat; it is more like a hotel room than anything else. Despite this, I have done my best to turn it into a home. I have built in cupboards to store the scraps of old material and slightly worn shoes which I have been accumulating ever since I was a girl – my motto has always been 'Never throw anything away if there's any life left in it', and with the exception of Paul Channon I have adhered to it rigorously. I also insisted on a proper airing-cupboard, since the radiators are too small to hang clothes over, and I don't think it's quite seemly for someone in a high position of state to hang their washing out of the window. I feel quite embarrassed when I look out over the back of the neighbouring houses and see what Mrs Lawson and Mrs Howe have put out to dry.

At eight-thirty a.m. it is time for me to go through my itinerary for the day with my staff, and I am usually in a meeting by nine-fifteen. Every day brings a different meeting; one day the Italian Ambassador, another the Education Secretary – or perhaps it may be someone really important like the Party Chairman or the election campaign manager. On Thursdays I do a Cabinet, which gives me a welcome break from the pressures of politics. Cabinet meetings, like the Changing of the Guard or the State Opening of Parliament, are one of those quaint traditions which I would hate to see done away with simply because they serve no useful purpose.

If I have time before lunch, I try to do a little shopping. Although I have plenty of backbenchers and junior ministers to run little errands for me, I like to take time to buy personal things (such as Denis's underwear) myself. I always make it a rule to get my Christmas shopping done in the July sales, and I can generally find something just right for everyone on my list – although I suspect that John Selwyn Gummer is beginning to get a little tired of swimming trunks every year.

I often have to do without lunch – a fact those who accuse me of being out of touch with the poor and hungry would do well to remember – since the middle of the day is invariably a busy time for me. Usually there is a factory to be opened or a hospital to be closed, and I travel the length and breadth of the country, from Land's End to Worcester, in the course of my official engagements. I am fortunate in that I enjoy travelling. If I'm not running up the country I'm running down the country, and I occasionally manage to make time in my busy schedule to meet ordinary company directors, bank managers, chief constables and other representative members of the public (my aides call this 'going walkabout'). I once even met an unemployed person (not counting Leon Brittan) and I was quite surprised. He was not at all like the unemployed people I had seen on the television, and he never once asked for money or tried to steal my purse. Incidentally, I would like to state here and now that the plight of the unemployed is a constant source of concern to me, and that I bear them in mind in everything I do, however trivial. For example, when during one election campaign we decided to show a dole queue, as an illustration of the inevitable results of a Labour victory, I insisted that we should employ genuinely unemployed actors to take part in the sequence. Of course, I made sure that their earnings were reported to the DHSS so that they could be taken into account when their benefits were next assessed. One has one's duty.

Occasionally, when the work of Government leaves me feeling exhausted, I like to relax by taking time off to attend a debate in the House of Commons. In fact, I spend a great deal of time in the House, one way or another. At a certain time every Tuesday and Thursday, any MP – even a humble backbencher – is allowed to ask the Prime Minister of the day (or, in my case, of the decade) for advice and guidance on any little problem which he may be concerned with. This pleasing ritual is called Prime Minister's Question Time, after the well-known gardening programme on the radio. I try my best to give helpful answers to all the questions that I am asked, although sometimes I do find it difficult to follow what some MPs are talking about. For example, there is a funny little Welshman who keeps trying to ask questions about the economy, and try as I might, I cannot make out most of what he says. Fortunately he is a member of the Labour Party and so nothing he says matters in the least. However, I am a naturally curious person, and this strange little person so intrigued me with his babblings that I asked one of my Cabinet colleagues to find me a copy of his manifesto. He had great trouble getting hold of one (it was a Thursday, and the dustbins are emptied on a Wednesday) but eventually he tracked one down in the British Museum library and brought it for me to see. It was one of the funniest things I had read in ages, full of expensive and useless things which the British electorate neither needs nor wants. Try to imagine an Argos catalogue and you will see what I mean.

Between five and seven in the evenings I usually have to attend a reception. Some people find receptions dull and uninteresting, but I regard them as part of my duty as Head of State – Britain's Official Receiver, as Denis once put it – and I insist on greeting everyone as they arrive; my wedding ring has worn quite thin in places with all that kissing! As well as politicians and foreign envoys, I often invite celebrities. To give you an example, I once invited Dame Edna Everage to a reception for a lot of other New Zealanders. I was astonished to find that she was really a he! I managed to disguise my distaste on that occasion, but I have to confess that I cannot be doing with female impersonators. Some of them, I believe, are married men, and it must put an intolerable pressure on their wives. Imagine discovering your husband is really the 'other woman'! Fortunately, Denis has never once tried on any of my clothes; he has too much sense. With his complexion he would never suit emerald green.

American actresses have always been a great favourite with MPs at the end of a difficult day, and naturally I am always delighted to welcome our American allies to my home. Generally speaking I get on very well with them, although I believe Miss Shirley Maclaine said that she got 'negative impulses' from me (perhaps she confused me with the electric light switch). Apparently she had the impression that we had had an unfortunate meeting in a previous incarnation, and for all I know she may have been right. She was probably one of the white mice in my laboratory when I worked for J. Lyons & Co – that would explain why her nose twitches.

Even at these supposedly friendly functions I find it difficult to relax. Unlike other people, I cannot sit down at the end of a long day and watch the television. The only programmes I have time to see are those which the Government is thinking of banning, and so I rarely watch for more than an hour or so each evening. Occasionally,

however, I make time for a really good comedy programme, such as *Yes, Minister* or *The Two Ronnies*. The
latter is a particular favourite of mine (I tend to be rather
highbrow in my tastes, I'm afraid) but I have often
thought that one Ronnie could do the job just as well.
And of course, there has only ever been one Ronnie as far
as I am concerned!

However, as I have said, most of the programmes that
I get to see are either obscene or subversive or both. I
remember recently a back-bench Conservative MP sent
me a video tape of a quite disgusting programme about a
group of homosexual characters all living together. Let
me assure you, I have taken steps to ensure that *Rainbow*
is never screened again.

As Prime Minister I have to attend a great many
tiresome banquets and dinners. Although I always have
my own speech to look forward to at the end, I find such
occasions rather dull, and one of these days I think I will
do away with them altogether. If I have to entertain the
Japanese Ambassador, surely it would be far more pro-
ductive to invite him to Number Ten, heat up a Vesta
chop suey in the oven, and have our discussion over a
relaxing cup of Bovril on the sofa, instead of having to
drive halfway across London.

Once the duties of the day are over, I can kick off my
shoes and settle down to an enjoyable evening of useful
work. I find that a ratio of five red despatch boxes to one
green box of Elizabeth Shaw mints is a perfect combination, and it is of course when I am on my own, with
no one to disturb or hinder me, that the real work
of Government is done. Although I realise that the
Parliamentary system is supposed to help me and take
some of the weight off my shoulders, I confess that it is
often more of a hindrance. However, it is the British way
and provides over six hundred precious jobs in the very
heart of the inner city of London.

Once the work is over and the nation has been safely put to sleep, then and only then can I retire to bed. I treat myself to a modest whisky and soda, which always reminds me that at least something worthwhile comes out of Scotland, and snatch half an hour with a good book. The temptation to read something light and frivolous after a hard day's work is very strong, but I maintain that self-improvement is a never-ending task, especially in my case, and so I always select a work of proven literary value. At present, I am rereading *The Fourth Protocol* by Bruce Forsyth, which is just as enjoyable the second time around. I have only one tiny criticism to make. The title is somewhat misleading – there seems to be next to nothing about procedure at summit conferences in it anywhere.

At last, shortly before three a.m., I roll back the covers and go to sleep, after a full but rewarding day of solid achievement. As you can imagine, I sleep very soundly. It may have been a day in which I cut taxes, curbed a trade union, sank an enemy battleship, slashed millions of wasted expenditure off the education budget, re-organised a nationalised industry or did any one of the countless things by which I make this country a better, safer place to live in; but at the end of the day I am happy to close my eyes in sleep, just as if I were an ordinary housewife who has spent the day scrubbing floors and ironing her husband's handkerchiefs. And that, I think, is the key to my character; I may be Prime Minister, but deep down, despite the power and the glory, I am above all else a human being, a woman and a mother.

CHAPTER ONE

A Child is Born

I have often thought how very fortunate I was to have
been born an ordinary person. It is to my childhood
experiences that I owe my unique insight into the hopes,
fears and aspirations of the British people.

I was born, on 13th October 1925, above my father's
grocery shop in North Parade, Grantham. I remember it
as if it were yesterday; there was no bathroom, running
hot water or inside loo, and one washed oneself from a
large jug on the bedside washstand. In fact, it was just a
very ordinary English home, such as millions of people
are happy to live in to this day.

My father – 'Mr Roberts', as we children affectionately
called him – was the eldest of seven children, and
although I never met my grandfather, Ebenezer Roberts,
I respected him enormously, as a treasured link between
myself and the splendid days of Queen Victoria's golden
age. However, my grandmother lived with us – rent-
free, for my father was above all a family man – and I was
not an only child; there was also my older sister Muriel.

The Grantham I remember was a busy, joyful little
community, where neighbours cared for one another and
everyone was happy to put aside a bowl of bread-and-
milk for the elderly widow who lived down the street.
Honestly, people would have laughed at the very idea of
what you and I call the Welfare State. Although I am
proud to have done so much for the Health Service and

the care of the old and inadequate in our society, I cannot help wishing that we could one day return to those happy days where people were prepared to stand on their own two feet and pull themselves up by their bootstraps.

Being a grocer, Father was a central figure in this community, for in those far-off days the small business-man, who has always been the backbone of our great nation, was still a force to be reckoned with. My father took his duty to his neighbour very seriously, and staunchly shouldered the burden of being a local council-lor, a governor of both the boys' and girls' schools, and a lay preacher at the local Methodist chapel. It was, after all, a time when the Church was still untouched by this terrible modern tendency to indulge in fashionable politics, and a man could be proud to call himself a councillor.

At that time, in the nineteen-twenties and -thirties, people were happy to serve the community in return for nothing more than the respect of their neighbours – and respected they most certainly were. If one thing more than anything else was instilled into one at an early age, it was the importance of showing proper respect to people in a position of authority: the bobby on the beat, the vicar in the church, the Prime Minister on the wireless, the factory owner in his mansion and those other unsung pillars of the community whose untiring efforts together make up what we call civilisation. Then, of course, we still had the death penalty, and nobody would dream of stealing, however poor they might be; if some high-spirited youngster happened to transgress, everything would be set right with a word of homely wisdom and a cheerful 'cuff round the ear' from the friendly policeman going by on his bicycle.

If you are a member of the younger generation, you may find it hard to understand the extent to which self-discipline was second nature to the children of that era. Perhaps I can explain this best by telling you about one incident which I recall very clearly. It was quite early on a refreshingly cold morning in January – I can't have been more than seven, I don't suppose – and I had the misfortune to slip on a patch of ice when I was bringing in the milk. Down went the milk bottle against the drain-pipe – I can picture that splendid old pipe to this day; it was British-made, of course, and tough as old boots – and it smashed into a thousand pieces. There was nobody about, and it would have been so easy for me to have hidden my crime by gathering up the broken glass and dropping it down the grill of the drain. But covering things up and misleading people has always been absolutely repugnant to me, and I can honestly say that the thought never crossed my mind. I stopped, stood upright, said in a clear voice, 'Margaret Hilda, you've been a *very naughty girl!*', and slapped the back of my legs as hard as I possibly could. It brought a tear to my eye yet I know that had I not done so I wouldn't have been able to look Father in the eye ever again.

In those days, of course, people really had to *work* for a living, and as daughters of a grocer my sister and I were very aware of this; in fact, I believe it was those early years among the sides of bacon and sacks of lentils that gave me my clear understanding of the fundamental importance of working hard and making one's own way in the world. A grocer, you see, is in a unique position to understand the dreadful effects of improvidence and extravagance. I shall never forget one poor, misguided woman who persisted in indulging her family's desire for butter, even when both she and her husband were out of work and could not expect to be able to afford such things. In the end, they were forced to leave Grantham, and their children ended up in the Foundlings' Home, of which my father was honorary treasurer. So, you see, it was my time behind the counter of that little shop that taught me the invaluable lesson that nobody, be he a humble factory-hand or the Head of State, can afford to spend more than he earns. Let me make this quite clear; you can't make tuppence three-farthings into threepence by borrowing from the IMF. To this day, in fact, when I attend meetings of the Council of Ministers I always seem to hear Mother's voice in my mind saying, 'Margaret,' (she always called me Margaret), 'God makes marriages but the tally-man breaks them.' These were no empty words, either; my parents simply couldn't afford to buy things on 'the never-never' (as we used to call it then) and it may well be that that was the secret of their happiness together.

As we lived in the little flat over the shop, the shop was always with us, a constant part of our lives. Perhaps it was this closeness to the source of our livelihood that taught us Life's golden rule, that one's work – if God has blessed one with His gift of work – must always come first. I smile nowadays to think that the wheel has come full circle and I am once again living 'over the shop' at 10 Downing Street. There are, of course, significant differences between the two establishments; for one thing, my mother would never have tolerated those dreadfully stuffy curtains that I have to endure in the main drawing room – within a fortnight of setting foot in the place she'd have had them all cut up for dusters. But when I suggested it to the civil servant responsible, he fobbed me off with lots of typical Civil Service red tape about their being public property and not mine at all. What nonsense! One thing I do mean to do is to fit a little bell over the door, just like the one we had in North Parade. That ought to put a stop to Nigel Lawson's incessant habit of popping round in the evenings to borrow a cup of sugar.

As a girl, my day started at half past four in the morning, when my sister and I would be up with the lark to do the early deliveries. After an invigorating tramp through the frosty streets, we would return home to see to the day's baking and scrub out the house from floor to ceiling, for we firmly believed in the old saw that Cleanliness is next to Godliness.

If I may digress for a moment, I was quite appalled the other day to see a certain bishop (whom I shall not name) surreptitiously eating gingernuts during a funeral service at Westminster Abbey. To make matters worse, when he had finished the packet, he screwed up the wrapping and threw it under his pew. When I was a girl, not only did we refrain from eating in church, we saved all our empty wrappers and sold them to the rag-and-bone man. Of course, it's so difficult to find suitable candidates for the episcopacy these days. Now I almost wish that I had chosen the other candidate they offered me, but I saw from his telephone transcripts that he was mixed up with Oxfam or some other subversive group and that was out of the question.

All the household chores had to be done before we could make our parents an early morning cup of tea and cook the breakfast. This pleasant duty would coincide with the sound of the morning post falling on to the mat as our postman, Norman, delivered the letters. Norman was a great favourite in our neighbourhood, with his cheerful smile and jovial wave. He had the misfortune to be born in Newcastle, but when he lost his job because of the rationalisation of the shipyards, he sold his pigeons, bought a rusty old bicycle, cycled down to Lincolnshire and worked for a while as a footman in the house of a local mill-owner before he joined the post office. I think my sense of fun always amused him. Whenever I saw him I would say, 'Uncle Norman, being a postman must remind you of home, mustn't it?'

'Why's that, miss?' he would reply.

'Because,' I would say, 'every morning they give you the sack.'

Then, without fail, the same smile would light up his face and remain there for a considerable time, and I would always hear him chuckling under his breath as he pushed his bicycle away down the cobbled streets. But back to my story.

Once the breakfast things had been washed and dried and the crusts of the loaf put carefully aside for a nourishing bread pudding later in the week, there was just enough time to make up the orders which customers had left the previous evening, peel the potatoes and warm my father's shaving water before running the few miles to school in order to be in time for morning prayers. It was a comfortable, settled routine, part of the happy family background that is the birthright of every child.

In every respect, Father was the source of my real education; but my first school was Huntingdon Tower Road Elementary School. It has been closed down now – by a Labour Government, needless to say – but I remember it as being a cosy little beehive of a place where teachers and pupils were united in the common pursuit of self-improvement.

One hears so much today about declining standards in education. What nonsense! I can honestly say that more and more money is now available, even in the State sector, while advances in technology have revolutionised teaching methods. Computers and microchips have virtually replaced the old slates we children wrote on with our little pieces of chalk – which we never threw away, of course, until our fingernails were actually scratching on the hard black top (a sound that I find unbearably evocative to this day).

It was also a different type of education. I dread to think what our teacher, Miss Broadhick, would have made of Ethnic Harmony or Peace Studies. I can remember her vividly, standing in front of the blackboard, writing, explaining and testing our knowledge – the 'chalk and talk' method, as we used to call it. I wanted to introduce a similar system into Cabinet in my first term, but a man called Michael Heseltine, who was then a member of the Conservative Party, threatened to resign if I did, and so my idea was shelved. So odd to think, all these years later, that by standing firm I could have avoided that silly misunderstanding over Westland!

Now I don't want you to think that all we did was gaze at a blackboard; far from it. How I used to look forward to Wednesday afternoons, when the slates were all collected in and we could start enjoying ourselves with some bonded numbers! Of course, with all mental arithmetic, there is the obvious danger that the teacher herself may not have the right answer. Even with a blackboard one can never rule out human error. I feel sure that Miss Broadhick, despite her many sterling qualities, had rather unsteady handwriting, and one would sometimes confuse her printing of 'two' with her printing of 'one'. I say this with confidence for she was often just one or two away from the correct answer. Being a grocer's daughter, of course, numbers were like a second language to me, and I recall with pride the first time that I was able to point out to Miss Broadhick that she had made a slight error in her calculations.

The decimal system was then little more than a notion in the minds of the French, and we counted in pounds, shillings and pence, as our fathers had done before us. Even so, I suspect that only we retailers truly knew how to think in shillings, which is why Father was convinced that any reform of the currency would damage his profits. 'Decimation, not decimalisation,' was his typically crisp comment.

Because of my knowledge of figures I was a wizard with fractions and strange bases – if you're under forty, you probably think bases are places like Molesworth and

Greenham Common, but of course they're really different systems of counting – and imperial measures were,
and still are, my speciality. I instinctively knew how
many ounces make a pound and how many gallons make
a peck. How many of today's GCSE candidates can tell
you how many ounces there are in a pound, I wonder?
And, you know, it's surprising how many people make
the mistake of thinking that there are fourteen when, if
they only took the trouble to look it up, they would
know that there are sixteen ounces in a pound but
fourteen in a stone. Even Miss Broadhick would sometimes need reminding how many drams made an ounce;
this was her blind spot, and I think the other teachers
teased her about it, referring to Miss Broadhick and her
frequent wee drams.

It was from Miss Broadhick, however, that I learned
the invaluable rule that a cake, even the nation's cake, can
only be cut up once; for she taught us fractions the
traditional way, using a circle which she would compare,
in her typically graphic and original way, to a cake. 'If I
give you the whole cake,' she would say, 'but then take
four-fifths, how many tenths would you have left?' Even
then, the question caused me some disquiet. Why *should* I
be left with only two-tenths, if it is my cake and I have
earned it? And if I am to be left with only two-tenths at
the end of the day, what incentive will I have to bake
another one?

The classroom, then, was always full and bustling. In
today's Britain, there are fewer pupils to each teacher and
fewer teachers in fewer schools than ever before; in my
day, Miss Broadhick had to cope with forty-five of us!
Since there was an odd number of children in the class and
the desks were in pairs, there was always one lucky soul
who had a double desk all to herself, and I must confess
that that fortunate one was me. However, I am proud to
say that the desk next to mine, although unused, was kept

as spotless as if it were my very own, and occasionally, as a treat, Father would give me a little dab of furniture polish on a bit of old rag to take into school to polish it with.

Discipline, of course, was very strict, which is how it should be. If the teacher had to leave the room, as Miss Broadhick occasionally did – usually in the early afternoon – a pupil would be put in charge and it was a great honour to be chosen for such a responsible role. If any child misbehaved I would write their name in a corner of the blackboard, and woe betide him when Miss Broadhick returned! In my first Cabinet meeting in 1979 I thought this would be a useful innovation, but nobody seemed to share my enthusiasm. I suppose they had a different system at Eton.

We took it in turns to collect the books and the slates and to be milk monitor, and when my turn came I would always beg my mother to let me wear my brown shoes, which I kept for best. Even then I recognised that if one looks good one feels good, and if one feels good one can cope with anything. Those brown shoes served me staunchly; but when my daughter Carol had given them a few years of hard wear I was finally forced to give them to a charity shop. I only hope that whoever has them now will derive as much pleasure from them as I did.

On a sadder note, I must tell you that Miss Broadhick began to fall victim to dizzy spells. To begin with, a mouthful from the small flask of water she kept in her desk would usually revive her, and her selflessness and consideration for others remained undiminished. 'Don't tell the headmistress,' I remember her saying one time, when a particularly bad turn caused her to drop all our slates on the floor. 'She has the whole school to worry about.' But in the end, her illness was too much even for her, and the little sips of water made her feel no better, or even worse. At times she would break off from her lesson

and start to tell us a story about a trip to Market Har-
borough with three of Kitchener's men just after the
relief of Ladysmith. We never heard the end of the tale,
for she would usually drift off into a sort of doze until the
bell for the end of the period aroused her. After a month
or so a new teacher arrived and we were told that Miss
Broadhick had left the area to look after her sick mother
in Boston. I assume that the Boston referred to was the
Lincolnshire Boston, not the place of the same name in
Massachusetts!

It was at school that my irrepressible sense of fun first
came to the fore. Although we were always a cheery
family and enjoyed nothing better than sitting round the
kitchen fire praying together or listening to my father
explaining about the Government, we had very little
time to spare in our busy lives for jokes or humour. My
father, I think, rather disapproved of laughter – 'the
Devil clearing his throat', as he once described it – and
my mother was not a particularly humorous woman,
although she sometimes smiled when my father went off
to council meetings. But in the more relaxed atmosphere
of the school playground, I began to develop that sense of
humour which has been such a source of strength to me
ever since. For example, whereas most children are
content merely to repeat playground jokes, I actually
sought to improve them – for I firmly and truly believe
in rationalisation in every sphere of activity – and
when once a girl came up to me and said, 'Margaret,
why did the chicken cross the road?', I scorned to give
the traditional reply. Instead, I looked her straight
in the eye and said, 'Because it has an inherent *right* to
do so. If it were a chicken living in Bolshevik Russia, do
you think it would find it so easy? Of course it wouldn't.
But in Britain anybody, even a chicken, has the liberty
to go where it wants, when it wants and to whom it
wants.'

I shall never forget the startled look on that girl's face! In fact, I was reminded of her expression in the early nineteen-eighties, when I was forced to dispense with a few Cabinet colleagues whose views were tending to drift away from the consensus of Party thought. You see, one must never be afraid of speaking one's mind, even in jest, although of course it's absolutely essential that one's mind be thinking along the right lines.

I also made up jokes myself. One of them became immensely popular, and I still smile when I think of it. It runs:

'What's black and white and red all over?'

'A newspaper?'

'No – the *Morning Star*!'

I have often thanked God for the priceless gift of humour, of which the above is only a small sample. You see, if one has humour one need never be at a loss for words, no matter whether one is talking to a Durham coal-miner or the president of OPEC – although naturally one cannot expect them to laugh at the same things.

Of course, life was not all school-work; there was always the knowledge that as soon as the bell rang at the end of the day, one could rush straight home to the warmth of one's family and the shop. I had only to lay down my satchel and carefully put away my school uniform – for we children were taught always to take the very best care of our clothes; 'it costs nothing to be tidy,' as my mother used to say, 'and an unpolished shoe is Satan's looking-glass' – and I was ready for a cheerful evening's work in the shop, occasionally popping out into the kitchen to do my homework and prepare the evening meal.

I like to think that I inherited some of my vocation to the public service from Father. I know that he would far rather have stayed at home minding the shop that he loved so well, lending a hand with the household tasks, or singing hymns with his family around the old pine kitchen table that my mother bought from the rag-and-bone man; but his sense of duty drove him out to innumerable committee meetings the length and breadth of our little town. As soon as the evening rush was over (or sometimes before it started) he would take his hat, cheerfully urge us all to be on our guard against shop-lifters, and set off on his round of civic duties. He never told my mother where he was going, in case she worried, but people used to say that he spent a lot of time with a widow who lived four or five streets away. How many councillors nowadays would take so much trouble over just one constituent?

During the week we rarely went out for pleasure – there was so much to do about the shop – and perhaps for that reason it was always a thrill when Sunday morning came round again and it was time to set off for chapel. I always think it is really imperative if one is engaged in public life to have a sound foundation in one's faith, and I shall never forget the almost magical feeling of that hushed little chapel before the harmonium burst into sound for the first hymn and Father began to address the congregation. He was an excellent preacher, and from him I learned the first rule of speaking in public, which is to speak up and speak clearly, and never to give way if anyone is churlish enough to interrupt.

For my sister and I it was also a wonderful excuse to put on our Sunday-best clothes, and the real fun always started at half past five in the morning, when the day's chores were finally done and we could take down our best dresses from behind the door, lift them carefully out of their newspaper covers, and put them on. My mother, who was an expert needlewoman, made a splendid job of altering my sister's clothes for me as soon as she had grown out of them, and it was from her that I learned the invaluable lesson that one should *never* press a hem, in case one wants to let it down later. Clearly, Shirley Williams's mother neglected that aspect of her child's education!

Then, in the evenings, we would gather round the fire and my father would read to us from the Bible. In those days, before the advent of television, reading aloud was much more popular than it is today; apart from the wireless, it was the main form of entertainment, and we rarely listened to the wireless, since my father did not approve of the BBC – he said that it was infiltrated by malcontents, Communist sympathisers and Fifth Columnists, so you can see that things haven't really changed all that much. Apart from the Bible, he would treat us to interesting snippets from the newspaper, which my mother would then iron so that it could be sold over the counter the next day (we could never justify the luxury of our own newspaper) and on my mother's birthday, he would take out the deeds to the shop from their tin box and read us little extracts, which he always rounded off by saying, 'There now, we couldn't have done *that* if we were renting.' There was one passage that we could never hear often enough; it started 'Whereas by an indenture of Conveyance dated the thirteenth day of November One Thousand Eight Hundred and Fifty-Six and made between James Elia Noble of the first part William Alfred Noble and the said James Elia Noble of the second part and Stephen Garnett Carslake of the third part it was witnessed that . . .'; and it got better as it went along. It was those readings that made me understand how important it is that everyone should have the chance to own their own home, even people who live in council houses.

Apart from the weekly excitement of going to church, there were other outings to look forward to. For example, from time to time my father would find it necessary to sue one of his customers for not paying his bill, and as a special treat he would take me with him to see his solicitor, a kindly old man who had his office over a tanning yard in the next street. I can remember my father lifting me up on to the big walnut desk, and sitting there swinging my legs to and fro while the two grown-ups talked seriously about such things as bailiffs and warrants of execution. Being only a child, of course, I used to think it strange that people should have all their furniture taken away just because they were out of work and unable to pay their bills; but when I asked my father about this, he would explain that it was his duty to my mother and my sister and myself, and that is a lesson that has always remained with me. 'There's always work for them as wants it,' he would say in his bluff, homely way, 'and if the blighters can't pay they shouldn't eat so much.'

Very, very occasionally, we would even go to the cinema, for my father, although by and large not in favour of public entertainments, had a weakness for cowboy films, which he maintained had a high moral content. I must admit that I tend to agree with him, and to this day I enjoy a good Western – little did I think that one day I would actually meet one of the really great cowboy actors, my friend ex-President Reagan! It was sheer delight for me to see Tom Mix as the sheriff triumphing over the villain and riding away from the camera into the sunset; and now, whenever I see a rear view of one of our wonderful mounted policemen on the television news, I find myself getting terribly excited and thinking back to those celluloid idols of my childhood.

When I was eleven, I won a scholarship to the Kesteven and Grantham Girls' School, where my sister Muriel was already a pupil. I can remember the proud smiles on my parents' faces when they opened the letter announcing my success; yet I did not learn until later the effort they had to make so that I could go there. You see, although I had won a scholarship, there was still the balance of the fees to be found from somewhere. However, people really knew how to make sacrifices in those days, and so my mother made do with her old shoes for a little longer, my sister took on an extra paper round so that we could pay off one of the newspaper boys, my father put an extra farthing on a quarter of tea, and somehow or other we found the money. It was then, I think, that I realised that one cannot truly appreciate the value of something until one has had to scrimp and save and pay for it oneself. Perhaps because of this, I find it hard to be patient when I hear people saying that the State owes them this, that and the other; if only they'd had to work like we did, then perhaps we shouldn't have so much complaining, and the waiting-lists for hip replacement operations wouldn't be so long!

Then as now, however, there were those unhappy individuals who cannot seem to realise that opportunities are for seizing with both hands and all your teeth, not for frittering away. I shall always remember one girl, who was a close contemporary of mine. Although fortunate enough to have been born with a good mind and of a sound Methodist family, she fell among bad company during her early teens and had soon lost all semblance of normal decency. Instead of walking to school like the rest of us, she persuaded her father to buy her a bicycle, simply so that she would have an excuse to go into the yard of the boys' secondary school, which was nearby, to park her machine in their bicycle shed (our school having no such facility). Such a course of action could have only one outcome; and shortly before she was due to matricu-late she was hurriedly sent to live with relatives in a remote country district, where her shame would at least be hidden, if not forgotten. Curiously enough, I came across her again only the other day, and as I could have predicted at the time, her life has been reduced to a state of demoralised abjectness. I shan't name names, of course; suffice it to say that she is now editor of the Woman's Page of one of our less reputable Fleet Street publications. There, I felt, but for the grace of God and Councillor Alfred Roberts, go I.

Those years at the Kesteven and Grantham Girls' School, then, were a magical time for me. As well as the academic subjects there were also exciting games such as hockey and netball, in both of which I captained the school, and the sheer joy of the school debating society, of which I was president. These roles were, I suppose, my first taste of the challenge of leadership, and to start with I must confess that I found them somewhat daunting. But I soon discovered the secret of managing a team, which is to keep everyone on their toes and fully conscious that their place depends on their willingness to pull together and follow the leader's directions. As soon as I got over my natural disinclination to drop people from the team because of their inability to grasp the true realities of a situation, I found that leadership is a skill like any other.

In particular I remember one very talented player who objected to the system of tackling the opposition which I introduced. Now the system was rough but fair, yet this person (who I shan't name) held that it was somehow unsportsmanlike and refused to have anything to do with it. It needed little thought before I resolved to do without that individual's talents for the common good; any team, after all, lives or dies by its solidarity, be it a hockey team or Her Majesty's Government, and the maverick individual cannot be allowed to jeopardise that. I explained all this at the next team meeting, and was pleased to find that pretty soon everyone was prepared to see the logic in what I was saying.

You may recall the incident of the broken milk bottle when I was seven. Well, I feel it is no exaggeration to say that ever since then, milk has had a rather symbolic meaning for me. So you will understand why I took my duties as milk monitor so very seriously. I soon found that the milk distribution system was in a terrible mess. Naturally, being a grocer's daughter, I couldn't bear the thought of so much inefficiency and waste, and so I hit on the clever idea of placing two straws in each bottle, which enabled us to reduce our milk requirement by half; and had I stayed at the school longer, I feel sure we could have reduced it further still. Even in those days I was painfully aware that milk does not grow on trees, and that cutting is merely a synonym for pruning, which is the essence of good husbandry. If only the French Agriculture Minister had gone to the Kesteven and Grantham!

Choosing the subjects one is to study at school, like choosing a Secretary of State for Northern Ireland, should be a process of elimination. For example, one should read English literature to widen one's perspectives and enrich one's personality, which is why I am so fond of Kipling. Becoming a Doctor of Literature, on the other hand, is plainly silly; as I once said to the Master of Christ Church, I wasn't aware that literature had been taken ill in the first place! Not that serious literary study is without value – as witness the notes in the margins of all my first editions of Jeffrey Archer's splendid works. In literature, however, as in so much else, I am entirely self-taught, and I have never found this to be a serious handicap; I am prepared to wager that I could work out who the murderer really was long before any of the grave dons I meet at High Tables the length and breadth of the land. And when one glances at even quite sensible journals, such as *The Economist*, and finds articles about things like Structuralism (which I must confess I took to be some new development in chemistry) one begins to wonder whether there is still more dead wood to be pruned back among the ivory towers of Academia.

Nor did languages seem to me to be a worthy field of study. I have never understood why the teaching of French occupies such an important place in the syllabus. It is such an illogical language, and my experience of the French has taught me that an illogical language results in illogical thinking. How silly, for example, to attribute a gender to a table! Perhaps my relative failure in French studies (I never managed to rise above second place) results from my inability to grasp this peculiarly Gallic concept. Now it so happened that at a recent EC conference the French delegate repeatedly referred to me as '*Madame* Prime Minister'. 'Non,' I retorted, 'as Prime Minister I have no gender. And as to being a madam I feel sure you have had more experience of that sort than me.' That wiped the smug expression off his face!

While I am on the subject of Europe, I would like to take this opportunity to correct a silly misapprehension that some people have. I am *not* anti-European. Some of my best friends are Europeans. For example, the other day I was at a function at the German Embassy, and I could tell at once that the new ambassador, a man in his late sixties, was clearly rather over-awed at meeting me for the first time, which is of course perfectly understandable. Instinctively, I knew what to do. As soon as a timely opportunity arose, I asked him what he had been in the war. He replied, rather shamefacedly, that he had been a navigator in a Junkers 88 – for those of you who are too young to know, that was a sort of German bomber.

'Fancy that,' I said. 'When I was a girl in Grantham, the next street but one was bombed flat by Junkers 88s. The aunt of a schoolfriend of mine was killed. Just think! That might have been you up there.'

After that, of course, we got on like a house on fire, if you'll pardon the pun. So you can see that a man's nationality means nothing to me, even if he's foreign.

Music of all kinds, from Gilbert and Sullivan to the avant-garde melodies of Andrew Lloyd Weber, has always been a source of delight to me; but to regard it as a potential career is plainly absurd. I dread to think what Father would have said had I ventured to suggest that his hard-earned money be spent on piano lessons! And yet I cannot help feeling a tiny twinge of regret that I never learned to play the piano. I have often pictured myself sitting at the keyboard, allowing my fingers to stray gracefully over the keys, like one of the characters in those adorable dream sequences in the old cinema musicals. In fact, I must take this opportunity to confess to a secret ambition that I nursed for many a year: the desire to be a motion-picture actress. Glamour and elegant clothes have always appealed to me, and I cannot help wondering what success might have been mine had I not been summoned by Destiny.

For me, then, science was the only option, and when I first encountered chemistry it was love at first sight. I revelled in ammonia and immersed myself in sulphuric acid; I was in my element, and I loved every second of it. Bunsen burners, test tubes, litmus paper and toluene had for me the sort of romantic attraction that I was never to feel again until I met my future husband. There can be few things to compare with the gentle fizz of dissolving sodium, the faery glow of burning magnesium, or the elusive perfume of manganese sulphate on a summer afternoon.

But I wouldn't want you to think that I didn't have a balanced education, or that I neglected the other core subjects. I worked hard at scripture, home economics and deportment, and although Latin was not formally taught at the school, one needed it for university entrance and so I learned it one Christmas holidays, happily mulling over the irregular verbs as I paunched the turkeys that we were to sell over the counter. And of course, no learning, however theoretical, is ever wasted; for now, when I hear political commentators saying that a Prime Minister should be *primus inter pares*, I know without having to consult a dictionary what the phrase means, even if I don't agree with it. The same is, of course, true of organised sports, with their tremendous character-building potential. I would like to see Leon Brittan coping with a bully-off and left-hand lunger of the sort we used to be adept in at the Kesteven and Grantham!

Soon, of course, it was time for me to decide what I wanted to do with my life. Obviously, the attraction of staying at home and working in the shop was very great, and I can honestly say that had that been my lot in life I would have accepted it gratefully and without demur. But both my father and my mother felt that I was cut out for some more significant career. 'The last thing I want is to have you on my hands for the rest of my life,' my father would jokingly say. He was always the first to encourage me to work harder and apply myself to my studies, even kindly allowing me to practise my maths by doing the shop accounts, and since he was by now chairman of the school's Board of Governors he took a particular interest in my academic career, to which I attribute my success in repeatedly coming top of the class. In fact, I remember him saying to me shortly after he was re-elected chairman for the fifth time and I came first for the fourth year in succession, that if it hadn't been for him, I would have come forty-fifth instead of first. Of course that was true, since without his unfailing interest and moral support, I would never have developed the moral fibre necessary for diligent study. My father was all the more conscious of the value of education because he had never had any formal schooling and had taught himself to read and write from the labels on marmalade jars.

Although I was fascinated by all the various subjects at school, I have always been a scientist at heart, and in those early days I could think of nothing more rewarding than working for one of the mighty industrial concerns which are (together with small businesses) the backbone of our great nation.

Surprising as it may seem, politics did not play a great part in my childhood years. Although I already sensed, from my success in the debating society, that I had many of the qualities that are essential to a statesman, I was yet to feel the call of Westminster and the challenge of government. But still, on looking back, I can trace in those early years the seeds of my later life. For instance, I vividly recall the General Election of 1935. My father was on the committee, and for my sister and me this meant many enchanting hours of filling envelopes and drawing up lists of names; and when polling day finally arrived, we were almost as excited as the candidates themselves. I can see my father now setting off in his delivery van to ferry some voters to the polling station. I remember being faintly surprised, since I knew most of the people in our neighbourhood by sight and I didn't recognise any of the men in the van, but my mother explained that they were all people who had been away for a long time and who had come back specially to vote. So you can see that in those days people took their duty as voters far more seriously than they do now! I can still picture my father coming home after his tiring day and stretching his weary feet in front of the fire while my mother unlaced his boots. My sister and I were frightfully nervous, but he seemed remarkably calm; and when we asked him if he wasn't afraid we might lose, he just chuckled and said there was little chance of that. He must have had nerves of steel.

Shortly after that, the situation in Europe began to deteriorate, and we all recognised the sad fact that a war was inevitable. The rise of Hitler in Germany was widely discussed on all levels in Grantham, from my father and his friends in the Rotary Club to the ordinary folk buying matches in the shop, and even we children could not help being aware that something was amiss. I recall, for instance, the day when my sister had a letter from her German pen friend enclosing a needlepoint swastika. My sister and I thought it was just a pretty toy, but as soon as my father saw it he confiscated it and locked it away in his trunk, with his Masonic robes. You see, despite the repugnance he obviously felt, he just couldn't bring himself to throw away something that might one day be useful for patching a hot-water-bottle cover or lagging the tank.

That, then, was my first taste of the pernicious effects of political extremism; and those of us who lived through those dark days will never forget the dread we all felt of war and the rising menace of intolerance. Chamberlain's promise of peace in our time cut no ice in Grantham, and I shall never forget the clear-headed, sensible way in which Father explained, when the situation was at its worst and the faint-hearted were starting to talk of giving up the struggle, that there could never be real peace without a strong military deterrent. 'It's just like the grocery business,' he used to say. 'If I didn't send the bailiffs in the moment someone's late with a bill, then your mother and me would be out in the street, and it's the same with this Joe Stalin and the Russians. What they all need is a jolly good hiding.'

When I heard that I had come equal first in the Oxford entrance exam, I was naturally overjoyed; I hadn't stopped to consider whether it would be possible for me

to go to university. In those days, of course, there were
no such things as student loans, and so I would require a
scholarship, or at the very least a bursary, to enable me to
take up my place at Somerville. All seemed lost when
once again my parents came to my aid. They realised that
this time it would mean unprecedented sacrifices; but
their staunch support never wavered. My mother volun-
teered to take in extra washing and do the rounds of all
three paper boys, my sister begged to be allowed to
contribute from her wages, my father put yet another
farthing on a quarter of tea, and so I was able to go. I can
honestly say that had it not been for their heroism, I
would have suffered a major setback in the pursuit of my
destiny.

I always say that although my father taught me selflessness, duty and the value of hard work, it was my mother
who showed me how to keep bread fresh overnight by
leaving it next to a bowl of milk (an example of practical,
as opposed to theoretical, chemistry which has always
impressed me); and so it was typical that her farewell gift
to me on that cold September morning when I set off to
start my first term at Oxford was a brand-new set of
buttons for my raincoat. I had often looked longingly at
those buttons, which had been one of the glories of our
small drapery counter, and there were tears in my eyes as
I accepted the brown paper-bag from her hands, realising
how she must have saved and economised to buy me that
present; but she simply smiled in her gentle way, said,
'Hurry up now, Margaret, trains and the Devil wait for
no man,' and went back into the shop to carry on with
turning the collars on my father's shirts. As I picked up
my dear old cardboard suitcase and started to walk the
few miles to the railway station, there was sadness in my
heart but also a great joy; although the doors of childhood
were closing behind me, the gates of womanhood were
about to open and I could see that when I came home at

the end of my first term as an undergraduate, things would never be the same again. My journey took me past many dearly-loved landmarks: the old workhouse, on whose committee my father had sat for so many years; the Methodist chapel with its brightly-coloured window; Mrs Potter's house, where that splendid old lady was sitting on the doorstep busily sewing away at the socks she darned to supplement her slender income; the Corn Exchange and the Labour Exchange, and the grand façade of the Conservative Club. Never had they seemed so beautiful as they did that morning, and I was leaving them, perhaps for ever.

Little did I know then, of course, what great things Fate had in store for me. But I feel that I can say, without fear of contradiction, that North Parade, Grantham, made me what I am today.

When turning out an old drawer recently I came across one of my school reports, which I reproduce here without comment.

KESTEVEN
AND GRANTHAM
GIRLS' SCHOOL

Name *ROBERTS, MARGARET HILDA*

Form *IV b*

Number in Class *Forty-five*

Position in Class *First*

SCRIPTURE   Position in Class: First......

Margaret's progress remains outstanding for a girl of her age. She brings an undoubtedly imaginative mind to bear on the subject, as her essay on the parable of th loaves and fishes proves. However, I would say she goe a little too far in saying that Jesus was wrong for feed the five thousand because they should have been prepared to go out and find work in other parts of Judea! Nevertheless, a fine year's work.

PHYSICS & CHEMISTRY Position in Class: First......

Another exemplary term. I only wish tha she did not find it necessary to drop beetles in the hydrochloric acid, as th is an expensive substance and th school's budget is not unlimited

FRENCH   Position in Class: Second.....

Margaret is an enigma. ~~For~~ most of the time her work is above ~~average~~ reproach, but sh continues ~~to let~~ herself down by making silly mistakes, such as using the first person plural instead of the first person singular in her French compositio

GAMES & P.E.

Margaret has once again proved herself a very able captain of the hockey team, although if she has a fault, it is impatience with the shortcomings of her less talented schoolmates. A captain should not find it necessary to reduce her goalkeeper to tears when she has the misfortune to fall over in the goalmouth, even if this does result in a goal being scored. Also she is inclined to be the teeniest bit 'bossy'. Otherwise, most promising

ENGLISH   Position in Class: first

Margaret has made extremely satisfactory progress this year, despite one or two disquieting tendencies. She does not take kindly to criticism, however gentle or constructive, & has been known to attribute meanings to certain words which they were never intended to bear. However, she displays a wide range of verbal skills for one so young, & her performance in the role of Herod in the school nativity play was little short of brilliant

MATHEMATICS   Position in Class: First

As her end of term result shows, Margaret is particularly talented in this subject; however, a word of caution should be appended to this fine achievement. Mathematics is an exact science, & she should not attempt to make figures say what she wants them to say when there is no foundation for her conclusion! She is also inclined to be a little argumentative in class.

HISTORY   Position in Class: 2 nd

Margaret would have been top of the class again this year had it not been for an unfortunate lapse in the last history essay of term. Her main fault has always been a tendency to 'know best', and she should be reminded that 'served them jolly well right' is not a satisfactory answer to the essay title 'Discuss the careers of the Tolpuddle Martyrs'. Otherwise, an entirely satisfactory year's work.

GEOGRAPHY   Position in Class: ~~forty-third~~

Could do much better. Has made no effort to learn what the principal exports of North America are, and either cannot or will not say where Liverpool is. This subject does not appear to interest her, and more application is needed.

DOMESTIC SCIENCE   *Position in Class:* First

Margaret is an absolute wizard with parsnips!

FORM MISTRESS'S REPORT

Once again, Margaret has justified our faith in her abilities, her overall position in the end of term results amply proves. I a pity that her personality occasionally verges on the <u>abusive</u> (!) particularly during the meetings of the Debating Society. I, she learns to curb her natural impatience with those who cannot keep pace with her, she might find it easier to make friends

HEADMISTRESS'S REPORT Margaret has had another excellent yea and her parents can be proud of her. Although she has not been blesse with universal popularity among her fellows, she has not allowed it to affect her work in any way. In particular, she has not been upset i the slightest by the quite unjustified comments made by some of the more irresponsible parents connecting her success with the fact that h father is Chairman of the Governors.

Margaret has once again won the Alfred Roberts Prize for Scripture Knowledge, the Roberts Grocery Mathematics Trophy, the Alfre Roberts History Challenge, the Roberts & Co. Embroidery Shield and the Alfred Roberts Spelling Cup.

SCHOOL NEWS
Thanks to the generosity of the Board of Governors, the chemistry laboratory has acquired a new set of Bunsen burners.
   The Chairman of the Board of Governors has most generously offered a new challenge trophy for work in geography, to be called the Alfred Roberts Geography Salver.
   Mrs Simister, the Geography mistress, is leaving at the end of this year.

CHAPTER TWO

Seeds of Glory

On a recent private visit to Oxford, I happened to be unveiling a bust of myself outside Somerville, my old college – quite a good likeness, if perhaps a trifle harsh around the lips – when I thought back to my undergraduate days there, and considered how far I had come from the innocent but determined young girl who stepped off the train in 1943 with nothing but her trusty cardboard suitcase, a sound knowledge of chemistry, and a dream.

I know it is all too easy to be sentimental about one's old university, and that sentiment can blind one to the less pleasant realities. I am fortunate never to have been afflicted with such sensibilities, and as a result the appalling present state of Oxford, infiltrated with undesirable elements and a hotbed of Communist subversion, has never caused me too much distress, at least on a personal level. A less stalwart person might have been wounded when, for example, a rabble of so-called economists conspired together to cheat her of a richly deserved honorary doctorate, and a mob of idle and over-funded students, nearly all of them doubtless using some nebulous arts subject as a mask for antisocial fringe political activities, crowded together to throw tomatoes at her when she opened some new science park. Goodness me! When I was their age, we were lucky if we saw a tomato from one year's end to the next. We would certainly never have thought of throwing them. Indeed, any food thrown at me I have collected together as food parcels for pensioners. But whatever faults I may have, bitterness and the bearing of grudges are completely alien to my nature.

It is many years since I saw Evelyn Waugh's *Maidenhead Revisited* on the television (Miss Waugh is so good I think she should be asked to write for *Howard's Way*) but I can recall the mild surprise I felt as I tried to square her curious description of Oxford in the nineteen-thirties with my own experience of the place a decade later. To judge from the book, you would imagine that every street was thronged with wealthy young men in the throes of hangovers clutching teddy bears. That era, if it ever existed, was long since over by the time I arrived. Mercifully, I found a university dedicated to the pursuit of learning, self-improvement and solid achievement – and this before the advent of student loans! Perhaps this was because there were very few men to be seen in Oxford at that time.

You see, it was the middle of the war and, with the exception of a few contemptible creatures who chose to hide their cowardice under the cloak of conscientious objection, every able-bodied man had answered the call of King and Country and gone forth to do battle with the ever-encroaching tide of Stalinism. The only exceptions were a few selfless individuals who, quite legitimately, had foregone the privilege of participating in the great crusade to pursue medical or scientific studies, in the knowledge that they could contribute far more to the common goal of worldwide peace by isolating a new vaccine or developing a new high explosive. Such men were to be admired, and indeed one of my own daydreams at that time was to stumble across some hitherto undreamed-of new variety of Molotov cocktail that would hasten the day when the boys could come home again. Alas! My experiments and research came to nothing, though the liquid explosive I was working on did turn out to be an excellent facial cleanser. I have that to thank for my complexion.

I rarely spoke to men during my student days; for one could not tell simply by looking whether a man was to be spurned as a coward or admired as a contributor. Even if he were the latter, I felt that anything more than a casual nod might cause a major distraction to his work and perhaps ultimately affect the outcome of the war. As a result I did not speak to any male student until May 8th 1945, V-E Day.

In fact, I must confess that I kept myself very much to myself. Not for me the idle chatter in the small hours of the morning over cups of cocoa that many of my contemporaries found so irresistible; my daily routine was inflexible. At half past five I would be up and dressed and reading through the previous day's notes before hurrying to Hall for my frugal breakfast – I have always found hunger a great spur to learning, and I often recommend it to many of today's students. Breakfast over, there were but a few scant moments with a textbook before it was time to bundle into one's gown and bustle off to the laboratory for the most important part of the day. Those happy hours of lectures and classes seemed to fly past like a dream, and all too soon it would be time to scamper back to college for the midday meal, in the knowledge that quick and unfussy eating might secure one a precious half-hour of revision before the start of the afternoon's work. And when the time came to wend one's way back to one's rooms and the library, one was suffused with the golden glow of useful learning acquired and study yet to come. That, of course, was the true magic of this enchanted time for me; the feeling that one could work and work and work until one's eyes would stay open no longer, with nobody at all to distract or interrupt. Oh, how I long sometimes for that golden age to come again!

I have always said that to surrender oneself entirely to pleasure is a sign of weak character, and since it was wartime everyone with a shred of decency was only too eager to do what little she could to assist the great enterprise that the nation had embarked on. Here, too, was a chance to vary the high academic life with a little earthy hard work, and I was fortunate enough to find employment in a canteen for American airmen; an occupation ideally suited to a grocer's daughter.

Recently I revisited some of those idyllic Oxfordshire bases, whose names are sheer poetry – Brize Norton, Bicester and Upper Heyford – and I am delighted to be able to say that whatever else may change, the sterling worth of the American airman remains undiminished. The occasion of my latest visit was our heaven-sent opportunity to assist my dear friend ex-President Reagan's crusade against the forces of darkness in Libya, and as soon as I set foot within the picturesque compound at Upper Heyford, I felt as if I were young again. I have already mentioned to you my weakness for American cowboy films, and perhaps it is in America's brave young pilots and bomb-aimers that the spirit of the Wild West is best preserved. I am not ashamed to confess that the tall, mysterious men in their leather flying jackets were somehow godlike in my eyes as I served them their rations of reconstituted egg and Spam.

As well as working in the canteen, I played a reluctant but wholehearted part in the various entertainments we girls occasionally mustered for the fighting men. It is not widely known, but God has blessed me with a fine singing voice – one of my few vices at Oxford was membership of the Bach choir – and when someone suggested that I might fill in at a concert for a girl who had unfortunately been struck down with a severe attack of dermatitis, I felt my duty outweighing the claims of self-effacement. The song that I was to sing was a pleasant little ditty called 'We'll Meet Again', and I can remember practising it in front of my little six-inch-square mirror on the eve of the performance. The trouble was that the tempo of the song was rather too rapid for me, and I resolved that, rather than spoil the song by singing it at breakneck speed, I would have to slow it down to a more comfortable pace. My insight was amply rewarded; for when, full of nerves, I took my place on the stage, I was greeted with the sort of applause that I was never to meet with again until I first addressed the Party Conference as Prime Minister. So enthusiastic were my audience that they insisted on clapping as I sang, in time with the music.

But even this did not satisfy my yearning to serve, and finally I took the plunge and applied for the post of ARP warden. It makes me smile to think that the image of that office firmly implanted in the minds of the younger generation is that derived from a television comedy series called *Dad's Army*, in which a rather vulgar person (astonishingly, also purporting to be a grocer) is portrayed ambling through a small seaside town bawling at the top of his voice. I was not at all like that. For one thing, I cannot abide having to raise my voice, as anyone who has heard me in the House can testify; for another, the duties of an ARP warden were both complex and demanding. However, I am pleased to be able to report that I rose to the challenge, and it is my proud boast that the area for which I was responsible was shrouded in complete darkness at all times. In fact, I was reminded of my efforts during the dying convulsions of the last Labour Government, when the electricians' union was permitted to strike and the entire nation was threatened with calamity.

I am sorry to have to say that I found many of my contemporaries at Somerville rather uninspiring people. One anecdote may serve to illustrate what I mean.

Shortly before going to Oxford, I had realised that my Lincolnshire accent, though by no means 'broad', would be a serious handicap to me in the realisation of my dreams. Many people would have accepted this disability without a struggle, but even at that tender age I was made of sterner stuff. So, when the last customer had left our little shop and it was time for me to sweep the floor and weigh out the tea for the next day's orders, I would practise my elocution. To lighten this load, I set myself the task of composing phrases that were designed both to train the voice and to educate the mind. You see, I could not bring myself to repeat mindless catch phrases like 'The rain in Spain' or 'In Hertford, Hereford and Hampshire'. Instead I worked out alternatives that had some moral or lesson to them, which I would recommend to today's generation; for example:

'Direct taxation means higher inflation.'

'Peter Piper pays the pepper picker a pittance.'

'Fewer schools build better battleships.'

'Nurses' pay keeps the voters at bay.'

Even today, when I feel a Lincolnshire vowel stirring within me, I find that these simple exercises, and the score of others which I concocted so long ago, help me to preserve the purity of voice which has been, I am sure, a major asset to me in my political career.

However, when I arrived at Oxford and found myself in the company of people still afflicted with palpable regional accents which made some of them frankly incomprehensible, my offers to pass on the fruit of my self-help were met not simply with apathy but with ribald amusement, and many wounding things were said behind my back by people who should have known better. That was, of course, part of the process of growing up, and it was then that I began to realise that there are some people in this world who simply refuse to better themselves.

Despite the sheer bliss of being at Oxford, I naturally felt terribly homesick for Grantham and the shop. Of course Father realised this and wrote to me frequently. Even when there wasn't enough news to fill a letter he would keep in touch by sending me one of the shop accounts to balance, and such was his concern for my well-being that at the end of every month he would insist on a complete statement of my expenditure of my allowance. I venture to suggest that few of today's parents would be so thoughtful.

I rarely heard from my mother, of course, since she was of a generation that still believed it is the job of the man, as head of the household, to write the letters. But sometimes she would add a little message to Father's letters, and I admit that my heart was touched when I saw her characteristic pencil cross with 'Mrs Roberts her mark' inscribed beside it in Father's confident script. My sister, too, never failed to enclose a brief note whenever she sent me money, and I usually did my best to snatch a few minutes from my studies to reply to her.

But these links with home were all too slender and fragile for someone who had always been brought up to believe in the family, and I had made up my mind when I arrived at the university not to allow the distance between us to become a spiritual as well as a geographical division. So, as soon as term was over, I caught the first train home and, pausing only to put down my suitcase, I would grab my apron and hurry to my place behind the counter as if I had never been away. Then there would be the joyful reunion with my parents, when I would hand back the small sum I had managed to save from my allowance, while Father entered the difference in his Loan Account ledger.

Our last family Christmas together was in 1943. After that my sister moved away from home to live permanently in Birmingham, working as a physiotherapist, and although this was a severe blow to us all, since we had come to rely on her cheerful presence and quite adequate salary, we bore the breaking-up of the family unit with staunch fortitude.

One memory of that Christmas will always remain with me. As I have told you, Father did not have the advantage of a formal education, but to the end of his days he continued to devote as much of his precious time as he possibly could to self-improvement of every sort. One evening, when the day's takings had all been counted up, I took them to Father to lock away in his trunk and imagine my surprise when, as he lifted the lid, I saw within a German grammar and a volume entitled *Build Your Own Wireless Transmitter*! Father could see that I had noticed these things and hurriedly shut the lid, nearly catching my fingers as he did so; then he explained that he had been extremely worried about the threat of enemy agents in the Grantham area.

'You see, our Margaret,' he said (he always called me 'our Margaret'), 'I reckon the only way to stop the enemy is to catch them at it. So when I've built a wireless set and learned their filthy lingo I can listen out on the shortwave and see if I can find out if any of them are at it round here.'

I have always felt that, next to the immortal words of Churchill, that faltering speech best sums up for me the indomitable spirit of the English at war.

Since I am on the subject of Father, I should add that he rose to the challenge of serving the community quite superbly. He was forever collecting food and other necessities for the homeless and the servicemen. That very Christmas, I recall, no sooner had he found in my suitcase a few bars of chocolate and a pair of nylons (a present from a kindly American airman at our canteen) than he insisted that I should contribute them to the collection he was raising for the Colditz Food Parcels

Drive. Of course I was proud to hand them over, and when I saw the heaps of similar articles inside his trunk I realised how tireless his efforts must have been. In fact, I do believe that collecting became something of an obsession with him, for a number of the things he had amassed, such as petrol coupons and the late Mrs Blackshaw's ration book could be of no conceivable use to our brave boys in German custody. But he was in many respects a simple man, whose compassion and sense of honour overrode other considerations.

Yet another blessing of my upbringing was that I was accustomed to going without; as a result, the shortages of wartime did not trouble me at all. I felt sorry for our neighbours, deprived of their accustomed Christmas luxuries such as goose, plum pudding and Brussels sprouts. But Christmas dinner that year in North Parade was the same as it had always been: a cheerful, frugal meal of bread and potatoes, washed down with clear water and followed by a simple dish of nuts and stinging nettles fresh from the park. These days, when we sit together round the table at Chequers and the housekeeper produces an enormous turkey and enough chestnut stuffing to fill the Channel Tunnel, I often find myself longing for a simple Grantham Christmas.

But sadness was never far beneath the surface in wartime Britain, and that joyous holiday was marred by one of the worst air-raids to hit our little community. Not only were two whole streets and the children's home completely levelled, but the small printing works in the next road, which was run by a charming little man whom we all called Uncle Rupert, was so severely damaged that production was halted for several days, and even the windows of the chapel were blown out.

Of course, Father was one of the first on the scene, almost before the all-clear was sounded, pulling away the wreckage and hunting under the floorboards of the ruined dwellings for any survivors. So single-minded was his desire to help that he seemed quite upset when the local bobby offered to join him, although his search was fruitless and all he found were a number of small articles, deed-boxes and the like, which he brought home with him afterwards for safekeeping and to pass on to the next of kin at a later date.

In 1945 and 1946 the officers began to drift back from the war and Oxford became bisexual again. I sat my Finals in the summer of 1946 and to keep distraction at arms' length, I continued to avoid contact with men. A less single-minded person might have found this difficult, for wherever one went Oxford was as full of heroes as Camelot. On every street corner one could hear tales of incredible valour, rather like the Cabinet Office during the Falklands War, and many emptier heads than mine were turned.

There was, of course, one exception; I first met him in the Chemistry School, where he was explaining to a fascinated audience how he had been fortunate enough to meet some German scientists during the occupation of Berlin who had explained to him the results of some of their medical research. If I may be permitted a joke, when our eyes met it was sheer 'chemistry'; for of course it was his obvious love for our mutual subject that attracted me to him. I immediately joined in the discussion, and once the others had drifted away our conversation continued apace. Imagine my excitement when I discovered that he was the son of the Earl of . . . But of course it would not do to name him. Suffice to say that he now holds an exalted position in the House of Lords.

Soon, almost inevitably, our conversation came around to viridium bichloride, and I could sense that as my mind unfurled itself before his eyes he was beginning to feel the first twinges of attraction for me. This was, of course, the very last thing I wanted; yet so intoxicating were his quite penetrating views on hydrocarbons that I found it difficult to harden my heart. Thus it was that, when he suggested that we continue our conversation over a glass of milk in the buttery of his college – he was, of course, a Balliol man – I reluctantly agreed. Had he offered me anything but milk, I would have been able to refuse; but, as you will recall, milk has always had an almost mystical aura in my eyes.

Every detail of that enthralling but dangerous half-hour is firmly etched on my memory; the teaspoons with Ball. Coll. engraved on their stems, the soft muttering of the college servants as they went cheerfully about their allotted tasks, the evocative smell of the furniture polish on the oak refectory table (how amused my companion was when I identified the brand as one we sold in the shop!). As we chatted idly together about such subjects as the growing menace of Soviet imperialism and the absolute necessity of Britain acquiring its own nuclear deterrent, I became aware of a strange stirring within me. Being young and innocent I took it for indigestion, but when we had parted and I was alone with my beloved lecture-notes once more, I found that bicarbonate of soda did little to alleviate it. It was then that it dawned on me that I might be suffering from something far worse than mere dyspepsia, and I recalled in horror that my thought-less folly had prompted me to invite the man to tea the following afternoon!

I must admit that throughout the lectures and labora-tory periods of the next day my thoughts were wander-ing, so that I caused a minor explosion by carelessly mistaking iodine for copper sulphate and pouring it into a strong solution of ammonia (for those readers who went to a secondary modern I must explain that this results in a highly volatile compound). Try as I might, I could not tear my mind away from my terrible dilemma, and I was still undecided as to what I should do for the best when it was time for me to hurry back to Somerville to prepare for my guest's arrival.

I had never entertained a guest in my rooms before, and I was quite panic-stricken. My first thought was to ask myself how my mother would cope in such a situation, and I was instantly rewarded with inspiration. Since I could not afford a proper tablecloth, I took a copy of *The Times* from the pile I was saving for Father and dabbed it all over with bleach to remove the newsprint, then hung it over the radiator to dry. I was able to borrow two cups and a teapot from my next-door neighbour, and a folded pullover made an excellent substitute for a cushion for my guest's chair. As for the meal itself, I had three biscuits left over from the packet that Father had given me for my birthday, and a few minutes' work enabled me to stick the pieces together with honey so that nobody would guess that they had ever been broken. A dandelion from the quadrangle in a simple test tube added the final touch of colour, and I was ready for my debut as a hostess. Although since then I have frequently entertained ambassadors, Heads of State and even kings, I do not think I have ever taken so much trouble to get everything exactly right as I did on that occasion.

My guest was absolutely enchanted by my efforts – he simply stared open-mouthed – but after a while the conversation dried up and I began to perceive that he was struggling with precisely the same internal debate as I was. Of course I understood; but there was a part of me that wanted to throw all caution to the winds, say 'Never mind about your career and your destiny!', and throw myself headlong into the world of reckless passion. Then, through sheer coincidence, our hands simultaneously reached out for the second biscuit, and I knew that the critical moment had arrived. That very instant, my eye fell on one of the pictures of Father on the mantelpiece.

It was a photograph of him opening the Alfred Roberts Ward in Grantham's refurbished Defectives' Home, and as my eyes met that firm, steady gaze I seemed to hear his voice saying, 'Now then, our Margaret, steady on. Life isn't all tea and biscuits, you know.' At once my hand shrank back, and I looked at my watch and remarked that it was high time I got back to my essay on petroleum derivatives. My companion nodded and immediately rose to go – for he was a perfect gentleman – and soon the door had closed behind him. After that, I occasionally saw him in lectures or leaning over a Bunsen burner, but we never exchanged another word. I can only hope that Time, the great healer, has repaired the damage to his heart, and that he has the comfort of knowing that his sacrifice contributed, in some small way, to the fulfilment of my destiny.

Of course, I had no inkling then that that same Destiny was in fact poised to overtake me. It was as natural for me to join the Oxford University Conservative Association as it was to breathe or go to chapel, but at that stage politics was little more than a delightful distraction from the serious business of study. As time went on, however, and I consented, rather unwillingly, to be president of the Association for a second term, I began to wonder whether I might not one day be able to devote all my time and energy to serving my country in this way. Such a dream was beyond my wildest hopes; but, as Father used to say, 'Those that don't shove don't get on the bus', and slowly the seeds of ambition began to germinate in my brain.

However, I must confess that I found the aimless socialising which at that time tended to play all too significant a role in grass-roots Conservatism not at all to my taste; there were interminable parties and receptions, which of course it was my onerous duty to attend. Oh, how often was I forced to stand for hours on end making small talk when my heart was in the library or among the capillary tubes! I remember one incident very clearly. A rather overweight young man buttonholed me and started off on an interminable speech about some book or other he had been reading – honestly, what do books have to do with Conservatism? The sooner we can put VAT on them the better – and my mind began to wander. Just as I was on the point of losing the thread of what he was saying altogether, he asked me how I, as a woman, found Austen's works. I immediately replied that I went down the Cowley Road, just like everyone else, and what did being a woman have to do with it? That quickly shut him up. Yet I fear that he was all too typical of the woolly-minded liberal Conservative that one tended to come across at that time, and which I have done my best to root out from the Party. One Lord Gowrie at a time is bad enough!

You may remember that I said earlier I had met very few effete young aristocrats who collected teddy bears during my time at Oxford; once again, there is an exception to this. I mention him now since it was through my Conservative Association work that I was unfortunate enough to meet him. At that time he was still called Anthony *Wedgwood* Benn and he was then treasurer of the Union – I remember that clearly, since it was about this time that the Union bar first started serving vodka (no prizes for guessing where that comes from!) and the price of a ham sandwich rose by 72⅓ per cent in five months. The Labour Party had just scraped into power in the 1945 General Election, and I can remember word for word the peroration of that ludicrous individual's address on this occasion.

'You see,' he said, 'I think what is essential on this particular issue is not so much the role of the State in society as the role of the State in creating a society which is beneficial for those whose role in society is, shall we say, more closely allied to the State itself. And that is what the present Attlee Government should be doing and what I hope and trust it will.'

You can imagine that this idiotic waffle filled me with rage. Although as a rule I strongly disapprove of barracking, however witty or constructive, I heard myself say, in an audible whisper, that the only society Mr Wedgwood Benn would ever belong to which would be even remotely constructive was a building society. Of course, it brought the house down, and the poor man grew quite red in the face, snapped the stem off his pipe with his teeth and spilt his pint mug of tea.

After the debate was concluded, I felt it was my duty to make my peace with him, and so I sought him out on the pretext of offering him a slice of anchovy toast. At first he did his best to snub me but I was determined to come to grips with him, and by virtually pushing the toast up his nose I was finally able to get him to acknowledge my existence. Soon we were talking quite amicably, and I was able to outline for him some of the more glaring flaws in his arguments. Fortunately, perhaps, his jaws were so completely glued together with the anchovy paste that he was scarcely able to utter a word!

Viscount Stansgate (as I shall always think of him) was not the only person later to become notorious whose acquaintance I made at Oxford. It was there that I first crossed swords with such deplorable people as Robert Runcie (who, even in those days, had a dandruff problem and stank of lavender water). His frankly treacherous behaviour since I made him archbishop frequently makes me think of Thomas à Becket and poor King Henry. There was also Frank Pakenham, against whom I canvassed at one election. Pakenham was later ennobled as Lord Longford, although the elevation entirely failed to reform him; in fact it seems to have had an entirely opposite effect. I am the last person to cast aspersions on someone's character, particularly if he is a peer, but I would like to hear his explanation of why some reliable friends of mine kept bumping into him outside seedy bookshops in the Soho area a few years ago!

Perhaps the crowning glory of my time as president of the Oxford University Conservative Association was when I attended the Party Conference in 1946 and saw Churchill in the flesh for the first time. In spite of the sniping of critics and the extravagant words of my sycophants, he remains for me the greatest Prime Minister of the century, and I like to think that our being together in the same room for one brief moment in time was somehow symbolic of the torch of true Conservatism being passed from hand to hand. Although we are different in so many ways – I have never smoked, for example, and I am sure Sir Winston never made a bread pudding in his life – in our determination to preserve our nation from the menace that constantly besets it and to make this a land fit for heroes to work in, we are essentially at one. Perhaps, then, this is the moment where the next chapter of my story should begin; when I was compelled by the beckoning hand of Destiny to leave the idyllic world of books and study and take my rightful place on the stage of history.

CHAPTER THREE

Ninety Per Cent Perspiration

During my years at Somerville the principal of the college was a rather peculiar woman called Dame Janet Vaughan, with whom, I must confess, I found I had little in common. Although she too was a notable scientist and an expert on radiation (a subject which has always been something of a passion with me) her whole character was flawed to its very roots by an unhealthy fascination with socialism. As a result, the atmosphere in the college was often distinctly unsettled and at times quite fraught; rather like the state of Britain before I won the 1979 election.

Since I firmly believe that one should not hold people's weaknesses against them, I only mention this to illustrate the unhappy fact that in those days at the end of the war a large number of people had not yet abandoned the Left, despite the terrible examples of its effects that could be seen right across the world. No doubt many young people who cannot remember those times will be shocked to discover that in 1945 the socialists actually won a General Election!

Perhaps this aberration – mercifully brief – by the electorate was what finally convinced me that I should listen to the voice of temptation that had been nagging away inside my head for many years, urging me to take up a political career myself. My experience in the Oxford University Conservative Association had shown me that

I was, by the grace of God, not only a Conservative but a leader of Conservatives; and in the middle and late nineteen-forties – in many respects Britain's darkest hour this century – I felt that I had a mission to do what I could to restore sanity to the nation. I imagine Joan of Arc must have felt something similar, although I suspect from what I have read of that rather overrated female, she was, like most French statespeople, fundamentally unsound.

But the dream was still only a dream when, in May 1947, I accepted an offer from a leading chemical company to work for them in the field of polymers. I was still young, and the urge to immerse myself in industry was irresistible; the glamour of corporate life, which I still feel to this day, glowed in my very marrow, and as soon as Father gave his blessing I wrote my brief letter of acceptance and bade farewell to Oxford. Because of some freak mishap in the marking system I was cheated of a First-class degree – I have never paid the slightest attention to the rumours circulated by some of my more zealous admirers that my political opinions had anything to do with what was, I am convinced, a simple clerical error – but I did not allow this to prey on my mind and beyond writing a few letters to the governing body and the newspapers I let the matter drop. I had done with Academe; it was time to return to the real world. I started work with British Xylonite in September 1947, my heart full of hope at this new beginning.

Perhaps I might take this opportunity to pause and paint a picture of myself as I emerged from girlhood into mature womanhood. I was, then as now, blessed with a porcelain-like skin, and I made the most of my appearance by dressing as smartly as my slender means would allow (although never flashily or gaudily; not even my worst enemy could ever accuse me of having disturbed the serenity of a navy blue suit with a fuschia blouse). It was, of course, the middle of the austerity period, and whereas those around me often moaned about the lack of colour and variety, I revelled in the tastefully drab shades and comfortingly uniform styles of the time. Being smart, I always say, is the main thing; showiness in any shape or form is abhorrent to me. A classic dark grey or black suit, a restrained hat, court shoes (but never more than two inches of heel!) and an appropriate handbag cannot, in my opinion, be bettered for a young woman who wishes to communicate seriousness of mind and a will to work.

My only concession to glamour was make-up. I had found that the Helena Rubinstein range suited me very well, and once I had made that decision I never wavered from it, no matter what the idle dictates of fashion might say. You see, I have always regarded loyalty as second only to industriousness among the virtues; not only loyalty to people but to the inanimate helpers of everyday life – which is why I always make sure my clothes are properly hung and put away before I go to bed. If you don't look after them, how can you expect them to look after you?

I found some suitable digs in Colchester, and the landlady soon became utterly devoted to me; she would even let me sweep out the hall and polish the front step once a week, so you can see what an impression I made on her. However, I spent little time in my cosy retreat. I had been entrusted with a responsible post in the research and development wing of British Xylonite, and I was determined not to betray their faith in me.

I was to spend three idyllic years in that picturesque little factory beside the gentle waters of the Stour; a period in my life which I often look back to with feelings of nostalgia. With no responsibilities to speak of (apart, of course, from repaying the interest on Father's loan) I was free to work as much as I liked. Unfortunately the factory closed at night and it was impossible for me to take much in the way of chemical apparatus home with me, but I did manage to collect enough ping-pong balls to build a model of the polymer I was working on, and many was the happy hour I spent pondering this or that nicety of atomic structure until my landlady's cat knocked one of my balls off and left me a carbon atom short! But this minor setback did not discourage me, and I persevered with my work on the bonding of hydrocarbons until I made several breakthroughs, which contributed in no small measure to the revolutionary design of plastic rainwear that was soon to be launched by my employers. I never claimed credit for my discoveries then and I do not intend to do so now. The knowledge that through my efforts of working in bondage the comfort and, in many cases, the very lives of generations of British people has been preserved is a sufficient reward.

I was also fortunate enough to win the respect of my colleagues at an early stage, to such an extent that behind my back they called me 'Aunty Margaret' and even 'the Duchess' (no doubt after the Duchess of Argyll, who was very popular at that time). As I approached my bench at the start of each new day, wearing my smart clothes and waving pleasantly at the lower-class workers in the outer laboratories, people would frequently cheer and whisper things to each other; and although I have never allowed adulation to go to my head, I must confess that I felt rather flattered by this obvious popularity. I did my best to merit it by sharing my knowledge with everyone who I felt needed it, from the lowliest assistant to the most senior scientists, and my colleagues soon stopped challenging me when we discussed technical matters and simply nodded dumbly, rather like today's backbenchers.

In order to reach the factory, which was some ten miles outside Colchester, I travelled each day on the factory bus, which our employers kindly provided for our

convenience. I enjoyed that journey; a pleasant few minutes with the *Daily Telegraph* (even then the only really
unbiased newspaper in Britain), from which I would read
out extracts to amuse my fellow passengers. Since many
of them were regrettably uncouth and backwards in
political matters, I used to read out the Association
Football reports as well as the leaders, but even this was a
learning process for me, since I became acquainted with
the names of a great many places, particularly in the north
of England, which I had never heard of before. The
beauty of some of those wild, remote northern place-
names – Halifax, Bolton, Manchester – haunts me still,
and it is my ambition to visit them all one of these days.

My social life in Colchester naturally centred round the
Conservative Association, where I formed what I called a
'39–45 Club' for ex-servicemen and women. Being determined that nothing but the best would do, I strained
every nerve to secure speakers of the very highest calibre,
and was fortunate enough on one occasion to be able to
present Enoch Powell (who at that time, before his lapse
into sentimental semi-liberalism, was very much the
coming man) to address our members on the role of
the newly independent colonies in the future of British
society. It was a most interesting address. Unfortunately
the poor man, as he often tended to do, allowed himself
to get carried away on a flood of obscure classical references, which many of my neighbours were quite unable
to follow. I remember coughing loudly to warn him that
he was becoming a little bit too obscure for the stout
burghers of Colchester; regrettably, the chairman thrust
a glass of water into my hands and by the time I had found
somewhere to put it, Mr Powell had completely lost
control and was reciting Latin poetry to illustrate his
views on how India should be governed. Of course, I
knew what *Parcere subiectis et debellare superbos* meant, but
that was because I had taught myself Latin. Most of the

audience were quite nonplussed. In fact, it was this speech that taught me that plain, simple English is the *sine qua non* of good public speaking.

You will have guessed from my description of myself earlier in this chapter that it was inevitable that I should have turned a few heads at this time; but since none of the many men who tried to scrape acquaintance with me over the retort-stands was likely to be of any conceivable use to me in my career I gently but firmly rejected their advances. However, one of these rather trying little incidents did have a happy ending. A Scotsman 'fell' for me at a Conservative meeting – I think he may even have proposed to me before a stiff talking-to showed him the error of his ways – but as I was preparing myself to put him out of his misery it occurred to me that a man like this, simple but honest, would make an ideal husband for my sister Muriel; she was reaching the age where it was imperative that she find a suitable partner quickly. On the next occasion when Muriel came to visit me, I introduced the two of them and explained my views to them as tactfully as I could. They were delighted with the idea and were married soon afterwards. They have, of course, been blissfully happy together ever since. In a way, I suppose, this was ironic, since throughout my childhood it was usually I who was grateful for Muriel's hand-me-downs and cast-offs!

In a typically Machiavellian and self-serving way, in 1946 the Labour Government had raised the salary of Members of Parliament from £600 per annum to £1000 – at a time when policemen were taking home less than teachers, I might add, and defence cuts were threatening the very safety of the nation. Little did the misguided Dr Laski (or whichever of those pathetic creatures it was) imagine how his underhand trick was to backfire – for I suddenly realised that it would now be possible for me to consider politics not merely as a pleasant hobby but as a career. I remember vividly the discussion I had on this very topic with a colleague as we prepared to extrude some polyethylene, shortly after the measure was passed.

'You'd make a good politician, you would,' she said, accidentally dipping her sleeve in the compound. 'Telling people what to do all day *and* getting paid for it.'

As I pointed out to her that she had added too much ethane to the mixture, my brain suddenly started to race and I imagined myself taking my place in the House of Commons! So great was my preoccupation for the rest of the day that I scarcely managed to complete my work, and I remember that I dropped a test tube, which unfortunately broke. But even as I made my way to the laboratory supervisor's office to confess my crime and pay over the tuppence, I could not tear my thoughts away from the vision which was haunting me.

But it was not until 1948, when the winds of fortune blew me to Llandudno for the Party Conference, that I was able to do anything about it. There, I happened to bump into someone I knew at Oxford; and after he had apologised, he happened to remark that he knew the chairman of the Dartford Conservative Association, who was looking for a suitable candidate. After I had reasoned with him for a while, he agreed to recommend me to his friend, and to cut a long story short I was later interviewed by the Selection Board.

You can appreciate how nervous I was when I presented myself for that fateful encounter. Father had most generously offered to come with me and lend me moral support – he pretended that he had business in Dartford with the captain of a small ship at Gravesend, but I knew that was only a white lie, since I was with them when they met and all the sailor did was hand over a small suitcase, which doubtless he could have sent by post; I knew that Father's real reason for coming was to look after me. With him at my side, I felt that I could face any trial, and my heart was high when my time came to face the panel. It was not easy, even so, for my fellow-candidates were all just as eager as I was to serve the cause. I remember that there was one man who offered to contribute £1000 to Party funds there and then! Fortunately, I was able to remind him that the Llandudno conference had passed a motion limiting candidates' contributions to £25. Nevertheless, it serves as an example of the commitment of so many grass-roots Conservatives of the time, when not only the large corporations but ordinary men and women dug deep into their pockets to pay the price of freedom.

As it turned out, I was chosen fairly and squarely by a margin of one vote, and I am pleased to be able to report that Father's staunch support was rewarded, for he managed to sell a hundredweight of sugar – which was still rationed and in short supply – to a local shopkeeper.

So it was that, in my twenty-fourth year, I set my foot on the first rung of a political career. When I think that so many 25-year-olds nowadays, far from having established themselves in the world, have not even bothered to find themselves a job since leaving school, I thank Heaven that I was brought up as I was, to stand firmly on my own feet and make my way by my own efforts!

Naturally, as soon as I had secured a candidacy in Dartford I knew that my happy association with British Xylonite would have to end. Although we had worked so well together and by our combined efforts made the world a drier place to live in, I think my employers understood my need to follow my vocation, for they put no obstacles in my path when I informed them, with a tear in my eye, that the parting of the ways had come. I dreaded the moment when I would have to break the news to my colleagues, since I find emotional scenes deeply distressing; but they turned away their faces and managed to hide their grief by covering their mouths with their hands, and I was grateful that there was no sentimental nonsense about leaving-presents or anything of the sort. Even my landlady, who had come to look on me more as a daughter than a lodger, made a feeble joke about 'getting someone a bit more lively for a change' as she helped me dismantle my molecular structure and pack the ping-pong balls in my suitcase.

I immediately found work with J. Lyons and Co. at Cadby Hall in Hammersmith, and took lodgings in what I hoped would soon be my first constituency. I have always maintained that a Member of Parliament should never forget that her first duty, after her duty to the Party, is to the ordinary men and women of the constituency, and that to live among them is the least one can do, however remote or bleak the place may be. I remember telling one young backbencher who represents a seat in the Midlands but who lives in Surrey that that was not the sort of behaviour I expected from one of my MPs. 'After all,' I told him, 'the voters have to live there, so why shouldn't you? If you want a seat in the Home Counties, you'll have to earn it, like everyone else.' It is of course a matter of deep regret to me now that I am forced to divide my time between central London and Buckinghamshire, and that I cannot see my loyal friends in Finchley nearly as often as I would like.

My work with the Lyons corporation was a great distraction to my political career, for it was intensely fascinating. For many years, the Lyons scientists had been grappling with the texture of ice-cream, and were on the point of making a breakthrough that promised to revolutionise the entire field. When I agreed to join the team, I naturally threw myself heart and soul into the matter, and it became a point of personal honour to me. As a grocer's daughter I had often considered the subject in a general way, but now that I was intimately concerned with the nitty-gritty of ice-cream technology,

I found that the substance had a deep, almost symbolic, attraction for me.

I believe that ice-cream is a microcosm of the remarkable organism we call the economy. When inflation is high and the world monetary climate is overheated it becomes runny and uncontrollable. When the money supply is restricted and protectionism causes the free flow of trade to freeze up, it is hard and intractable, and one needs all one's strength to scoop it out of the carton. But when everything is correctly modulated and all the external factors are under the firm control of a stalwart American president, it becomes soft and pliable yet firm and solid; and in those rare moments of history when the nations unite in common understanding, it takes on an ethereal quality, I might almost say a fluffiness, which beggars all description. Ice-cream, in its cold loveliness, has always been an inspiration to me, and for that I have my Hammersmith period to thank. Modesty forbids me to enlarge on my achievements in the field of ice-cream research, not to mention my trail-blazing work on cake-fillings; suffice it to say that when the pudding is served at the Mansion House dinner I often feel a glow of internal satisfaction at the thought that it is not only as a politician that I have enriched the lives of so many people. My only regret is that by making cake irresistible to the nation, Nigel Lawson is six stone heavier than he might otherwise be.

This fulfilling challenge stimulated me in my political work, and as I arrived back in Dartford after a day's work to begin an evening of canvassing, I felt an inner peace. I have always loved canvassing – the thrill of knocking on some ordinary person's door with the prospect of an opportunity to communicate one's beliefs to a total stranger – and now that I was canvassing on my own behalf I could scarcely bring myself to go home at night. However, the stark reality of the situation was that the socialist candidate, a funny little man called Norman Dodds, had a majority of over 20,000. Had I been selected earlier, I feel that I might have succeeded in converting Dartford, for they were basically decent people, at heart. But even I could not knock on every door in the short time at my disposal, and as the election drew nearer I could sense that this time victory was likely to elude me. I was not deterred, however, and with nothing to lose I was uniquely able to enjoy the lighter side of the campaign.

I found that by canvassing early in the morning, between six and half past seven, I was not only able to take advantage of what would otherwise have been time wasted in sleep but to catch many voters at home whom I would otherwise have missed. It never ceases to amaze me, by the way, how so many people fritter away so many hours of their lives by sleeping in in the mornings. I have always been an early riser, ever since I was a child, and I always say that if I live to be ninety I shall have lived 98,550 hours longer than a person of a similar age who has never got up before seven o'clock! Everyone I say this to sees the force of my argument, particularly when I go through the figures for them on the back of an envelope or menu card, but even so most of them persist in their sluggish ways, as I have often noticed when telephoning Cabinet colleagues before breakfast. Unfortunately, so far the Parliamentary timetable has been too full for me to be able to tackle this serious waste of human resources by legislation, but I have not yet abandoned hope by any means.

The only people, then, whom I used to meet as I went my rounds were such humble folk as postmen, milkmen and dustmen, and I got to know several of them quite well. There was one particular dustcart whose crew were always ready with a cheery wave when they saw me coming with my pamphlets under my arm, and they always made a joke of sorts about how different our occupations were since they were *collecting* rubbish. To this day, I don't quite understand the point of the joke – I think what they were driving at is that they were collecting rubbish while I was collecting votes.

Having been brought up in Grantham, which was a rather more – how shall I say? – salubrious area than Dartford, I tended to find that I had a little difficulty in understanding what some of the voters were saying. I soon learned to cope with this by smiling brightly no matter what, and I have found that this is an excellent way of coping not only with voters but with foreigners and sporting celebrities too. Each day before setting out I used to stand in front of the mirror and practise my smile and my caring face (a habit I have retained to this day) and thus armed I was quite irresistible to the electorate. But oh! how wearing it can be, smiling for hours on end, particularly if you have the misfortune to be faced with a socialist!

One of the great controversies of the 1950 General Election centred round a picture on the front page of an obscure little newspaper called the *Daily Mirror* (I believe it is still in existence, although I haven't seen a copy for years), which showed a gun ready to shoot and bore the caption 'Whose Finger On The Trigger?'. It was explained to me that this was meant as a cheap jibe at Sir Winston Churchill's firm stand on the Cold War issue, and although I felt sure that any voter with a scrap of common sense would treat it with the contempt it deserved, I saw how it could be used to my own advantage. When the next election meeting came round, I turned to face the audience and asked them, 'Do you want to know whose finger should be on the trigger? I'll tell you whose. Mine!' And then I waved my finger at them and said, 'Because there's more sense in this finger than in the whole of the Labour Party put together.' Of course the rowdies at the back (whom I strongly suspect had been hired from the public houses an hour or so earlier) began making noises and booing; but the more they booed the more I waved my finger, until I dislocated something in my wrist and it became quite painful. But I wasn't to be beaten, and when they found that I could shout just as loud as they could, in fact considerably louder, they soon gave up and left the hall, and I was able to continue my address in peace and quiet. Ever since then, however, I have had a tendency to rheumatism in that hand, for which I hold the *Daily Mirror* entirely to blame.

Thanks to my hard work, I was able to reduce the socialist majority by a thousand votes in the by-election, and by a further thousand in the General Election of 1950. But this was slow progress and when I told Father the result he said that at that rate it would be 1970 before I became an MP. I corrected his arithmetic (he should have said 1968), but his words made a deep impression on me and I began to consider whether my loyalty to Dartford had been misplaced. After all, loyalty is only a virtue if it is reciprocated, as I told Jim Prior when I sent him to Northern Ireland, and it occurred to me that I would be better advised to direct my loyalty towards a constituency who would deserve it. At that time, of course, Finchley was only a name to me; little did I know that it would one day be to me what Avalon was to King Arthur!'

Although Dartford was a disappointment, it was the crucible of my destiny in more ways than one. Not only was I blooded as a politician, I also met someone who, second only to Father, has influenced me more than anyone else. We met on the evening of the adoption meeting in 1949. Denis Wilberforce Thatcher, as he then was, belonged to the local Conservative Association. He was a prominent local businessman and a pillar of the community, the sort of man (I say this without fear or favour) who has made this country what she is today. He too had made his own way in the world, taking over the managing directorship of the family firm from his father at a comparatively early age and building it up by his own unaided efforts. As he told me the story of his latest boardroom battle, he seemed a terribly romantic and glamorous figure, shrouded in the mystique of the successful entrepreneur; I can best explain it by saying that Rupert Murdoch reminds me very much of Denis Thatcher when I first knew him. He has that same cool, businesslike brain beneath a rugged, manly exterior, that same thrilling combination of ice and fire. But I digress.

When he had finished telling me his story, he smiled and offered me a drink, which I blushingly refused. Then, like young people of every age who sense the first stirrings of warm feeling, we began to talk about the stock market. I could see that he was attracted to me, since he almost immediately offered to sell me some shares he had recently acquired in a West African goldmine, which he assured me was likely to be tremendously successful in the very near future. I was touched and flattered, and I only wished that I could have afforded to accept his offer, for even then I was committed to the ideal of wider share ownership. But it so happened that I had just paid Father the latest instalment of interest on his loan, and I was virtually penniless. Characteristically, Denis was not at all hurt by my refusal and we started to talk about the election instead. Then he went to the bar for another drink and it appeared that he had lost interest in me, since I saw him talking excitedly to someone else. But, as I was preparing to leave he came back and, in his typically amusing fashion, pretended to have forgotten that we had already met, introducing himself again. As he said, 'Hello, I'm Denis Thatcher, who are you?' I could not prevent a little smile crossing my lips, for I had never met anyone with such a subtle sense of humour.

After we had chatted for a little while about Keynes and the fallacy of direct taxation, I said that it was time I was getting back, since I had to get to Liverpool Street in time for the last train. He pretended that I had said Liverpool and was quite unbearably amusing, and when I had explained for the third time he offered to drive me there. A mad, devil-may-care impulse seized me and I accepted.

It was only to be expected that someone so dashing should drive a Jaguar, and although it broke down on the way and I lost the heel of my only pair of evening shoes pushing it down Ludgate Hill, I was completely swept off my feet. My heart was in my mouth as I said goodnight, and to my joy Denis asked if he could see me again.

It was, if you'll pardon the cliché, a whirlwind romance. I soon learned all about him. He had been a major in the Royal Artillery during the war, and had won himself imperishable glory for an act of conspicuous bravery; he had rescued his unit's only rugby ball when it sailed over the lines following an unsuccessful attempt at a drop-goal and landed in a German machine-gun nest.

He had been married before but his first marriage had ended in divorce. Of course, Denis had been the injured party. I remember tears of sympathy springing to my eyes when he told me the story of the final breakdown. His ex-wife had been caddying for him during a thunderstorm, and she deliberately handed him a five-iron instead of a putter for a delicate trickle into the hole. He only discovered her treachery when the head of the club connected with the ball, and by then of course the mischief had been done. Had it not been for that, he told me, he would have potted a birdie. He didn't say what sort of birdie, but I imagine it was a pheasant or a grouse.

Even then, he had tried to repair the damage, going so far as to speak to her on the drive home. But she persisted in her pettiness and used metal polish instead of mineral oil to clean his steel-shafted drivers, nearly ruining them in the process. This was more than flesh and blood could stand, and Denis filed for divorce the next day.

When I met him he was thirty-six years old, with his own flat in Swan Court in Chelsea, a little pied-à-terre on the Isle of Man, and an apartment in Johannesburg only a drop-kick away from Newlands, the home ground of his beloved Springboks. He was, it goes without saying, a Conservative and a Methodist; so, despite his divorce, I felt reasonably confident that I could win Father's approval for my choice.

When we arrived in Grantham for that decisive meeting, Father was in the upstairs room doing the books. I was so excited at bringing my future husband home to see my parents that I thoughtlessly burst into the room without knocking. Father must have been greatly alarmed, for he jumped and accidentally upset his big ledger so that it fell down behind the desk.

'Now then, our Margaret,' said Father, 'you didn't half give me a turn. In fact, I could do with a spot of medicinal brandy.'

Here was a chance for Denis to win Father's approval at once, and he did not neglect it. 'As it happens, Mr Roberts,' he said, stepping forward and reaching into his pocket, 'I have a small flask of medicinal gin with me. Would you care for a . . . ?'

So deep an impression did Denis's simple act of chivalry make on Father that from that moment they were firm friends. In fact, they were so taken with each other that I saw very little of them during that visit; they would either be sitting upstairs talking about something or other, deep into the night, or else Father would take Denis out to meet his friends on the Round Table, and they would not return from their charitable work until I had gone to bed – indeed, on the third morning of the visit, they were huddled on the doorstep when I went down at ten to five to open the shop. Obviously they had both been working so hard at some good cause or other that they had fallen asleep before Father could unlock the door. Father liked Denis so much that he even sold him his precious old Russian Government Bonds, which I think he had bought before the First World War and which clearly had great sentimental value for him. Looking back, I think that those bonds were meant as my 'dowry', and when Denis eventually found out that they were worthless, neither of us had the heart to tell Father for fear of hurting his feelings.

Denis's proposal to me, like everything else he did, was spontaneous and unconventional. I had long enjoyed knitting, and it had occurred to me that he might like some little cosies to go on the heads of his golf-clubs. The only problem was that I couldn't find a pattern, and I felt terribly frustrated until one day I had the brilliant idea of using a pattern for babies' bootees. I set to work at once, using pink wool for the steel-shafted drivers and blue for the woods, and I was absent-mindedly knitting away while I was waiting for Denis to come and take me to see the Springboks play at Twickenham. When Denis arrived, I forgot to hide my surprise, and he saw the little bundle on the chair. He must have guessed what I was doing and the kind thought spurred him into action, for he proposed on the spot. Needless to say I accepted without a moment's hesitation and I have not wavered in my commitment one jot ever since.

We were married on 13th December 1951 at the Wesleyan chapel, City Road, in the East End of London. Every detail of that day is firmly stamped on my consciousness; the telegrams, the flowers, the wireless commentary on the 'Varsity match which Denis insisted we had on at the reception, and the fascinating report on Australian interest rates in that morning's *Telegraph*. Since Denis had been married before, it was obviously out of the question for me to wear a traditional wedding dress, and so I chose a smart, formal outfit which I would be able to wear to work. I was most particular about it, and took the biscuit-tin lid on which I had seen the design – by a man called Joshua Reynolds, who seemed to specialise in biscuit tins – to the dressmaker with instructions that she should copy it exactly. Imagine my horror when I turned up for my first fitting and realised that the idiotic woman had copied the wrong picture and had made me a set of hunting pinks, complete with brass buttons! But my mother came to my rescue, and for the next forty-eight hours she worked nonstop, cutting the complicated pattern out of a pair of old parlour curtains which she had put away for just such an emergency when I was twelve.

The fateful day came and Denis and I stood nervously before the minister (it's odd to think that today ministers stand nervously before *me*). At least, I was nervous; I think Denis's mind was elsewhere, for he seemed to be doing mathematical calculations under his breath. As the momentous question was put to me, I suddenly felt a moment of doubt. I remember asking myself, in that split second, 'Should I take this man to be my lawful wedded husband? Margaret Hilda, you've never *taken* anything in your life before; you've always *given*. Should you really take something that doesn't belong to you? Shouldn't you earn it instead?' But the 'No' in my head was overwhelmed by the 'Yes' in my heart, and all my doubts were swept aside by one word from the minister. That word, of course, was *lawful*. We all have a duty to uphold the law, whether we be politicians, policemen or even the ordinary man on the football terraces, and I realised then that by saying 'Yes' I would be contributing in no small measure to the civilised way of life which we in Britain are proud to call democracy.

Our honeymoon was in Rome and then Paris; Denis

had originally arranged a trip to Pietermaritzburg, where the Springboks were playing the All Blacks, but there was a mix-up in the bookings and we had to settle for second best. It was the first time I had ever been abroad; little did I think as I walked through the streets that one day I would be visiting these great cities as my country's head of state. And yet, especially in Paris, I felt somehow at home, and I attribute this to the fact that I paid attention to my history lessons at school. I remembered that for many hundreds of years France was just as much a possession of the British crown as, for example, York-shire (in some ways more so) and that the claim to the French throne was not officially renounced until the reign of George III. One day, perhaps, when the Channel Tunnel is complete, we may yet regain our French dominions and then we won't have to stand any more of this nonsense about wine lakes and butter mountains!

Denis too seemed perfectly at home abroad, although he seemed to prefer Italy, where he had been in the war; I remember how he stopped in the ruins of the Coliseum to point out to me where the goalposts had been pitched when he scored a try against a scratch Australian team. I shall always recall those sunny days in Rome, basking at the foot of Trajan's Column reading my little book on purchase tax while Denis toyed with a glass or two of a local soft drink called chianti and explained the rules of golf to me over and over again. Yet both of us knew that it was only a short interlude before we returned to the harsh but invigorating demands of our respective destinies. Before me was a new ambition, which my marriage had made possible – a new line of attack on the citadel of Westminster. Something Denis had said, about there being very few really sharp lawyers about these days, had reminded me of a chance remark of a family friend shortly after my father became Mayor of Grantham, and I had made up my mind to read for the Bar.

It was always my habit as a girl to do my homework on the kitchen table, and our little kitchen was next door to the parlour, where my father entertained his friends from the council. At the time, my father was terribly busy with some great new housing project, and I remember that I was sitting by the fire and glancing through a new chemistry book I had been given for my birthday when I overheard my father and some colleagues of his, who I think were important local builders, talking in the next room.

'When folk hear of this, Alf,' joked one of them, 'you'll wish you had a good lawyer in the family, instead of just a chemist and a daft physiotherapist.'

So it was that when I returned to England from my honeymoon it was not simply as a married woman; it was also as a fledgling barrister.

Wife, mother, politician, leader – and author!

We are a grandmother.

Duty-free shopping in Namibia.

The early bird . . .

'The lady's not for turning.'

Parting is such sweet sorrow.

There is some corner of a South Atlantic field that is
forever England.

'Britain has sufficient fossil fuel for two centuries.'
Ministry of Energy Report 1986

I relish the drama of an all-night sit-in.

I 'Feed The World' tuppence a bag.

I too am a Young Conservative.

V is for victory 1979/1983/1987.

CHAPTER FOUR

A Mother's Joy

Hardly a day passes without someone, a journalist or biographer or just an ordinary voter, asking me which, of all my many achievements, gives me the most pride and satisfaction: my unwearied battle against inflation, my steadfast resistance to the growing menace of Soviet imperialism and trade union power, my single-handed restoration of law and order, or my successful conquest of the unemployment problem?

You would think, wouldn't you, that I would find it hard to answer such a question. But in fact, the answer that I always give is none of these. My proudest boast is that, throughout my political career, I have always been a good wife and mother and have never – *never* – wasted food. In fact, I can honestly say that even now a stale crust safely converted into a nourishing bread pudding gives me more pleasure than thirty thousand off the un-employment total. How many Prime Ministers in this or any other century could say that, I wonder?

You see, when I returned from my fairytale honey-moon a married woman, it was with the knowledge that, thanks to Denis's financial acumen, I need never work again. But the difference between 'needn't work' and 'won't work', as I so often tell the young men and women fortunate enough to have places on a YTS scheme, is the difference between virtue and sin. One has only to look back to the Victorian era, when Members of

Parliament were unpaid, to realise that most of the great statesmen in history have been sufficiently comfortably off not to have had to work: Gladstone, Curzon, even Boadicea herself.

So, although I had already enrolled with the Council for Legal Education as the first stage to furthering my political ambitions through the Bar (the Bar, by the way, is a technical term we lawyers use for the barrister's profession, and nothing at all to do with public houses; although many of the scenes I have witnessed in courts the length and breadth of Britain would make you think otherwise) nevertheless I knew that my first duty was to make sure that Denis always came home to a hot, nutritious meal and had a clean shirt and properly darned socks to wear to work in the morning.

In fact, my legal studies gave me ample time to combine work with the pleasure of running a household. I spent many an enchanted afternoon with a darning-needle in one hand and Winfield and Jolowicz on Tort in the other, glancing backwards and forwards from *Volenti non fit injuria* to the leeks simmering merrily on the hob. On one occasion, I remember, I got so carried away that I embroidered the whole *ratio decidendi* of *Proctor v Bayley* on one of Denis's golfing sweaters before I realised what I was doing!

My pupillage as a barrister was, I must confess, a rather frustrating time for me, since it soon became apparent that I knew far more law than any of the so-called 'qualified' barristers around me. However, by correcting their errors and giving them the benefit of my advice whether they asked for it or not, I quickly won their respect and admiration and was given a great deal of important research work to do in a room of my own at the far end of the building where I could not be distracted by people passing by and chattering.

Once my pupillage was over, I knew that I need no

longer rely on Denis's unstinted generosity – like my father before him, he had lent me every penny I needed for the expenses of my training, at less than the prevailing interest rate – and could now stand on my own two feet again. Naturally, I did not allow my financial independence to blind me to my duty as a wife, and I was always careful to be home in plenty of time to have the evening meal ready: bacon and egg Mondays to Thursdays, and sausage and tomato the rest of the week, with plenty of fried bread to wipe up the delicious juices, while on special occasions, such as Denis's birthday or Empire Day, I would throw caution to the winds and there would be a steamed pudding or plum duff to follow. Denis, in his characteristically chivalrous way, tried to take some of this burden from my shoulder by dining out once or twice a week with business colleagues, but his self-sacrifice was not necessary, for my upbringing had trained me to take responsibilities of this kind in my stride.

I took a tenancy in chambers at 5 King's Walk in the Inner Temple, where I found that my knowledge of chemistry led me inexorably to work in the field of patents. It has been a source of joy to me that throughout my life I have always been lucky enough to do work that is in itself useful to society. While those around me were wasting their lives with divorce cases or defending criminals who were obviously guilty – a practice which I have always found repugnant, and which I am doing something to prevent – I was able to continue to contribute towards the industrial growth of our nation.

Britain has always been a nation of inventors, from the earliest times down to Sir Clive Sinclair, and the patents lawyer naturally spends a large proportion of her time in the company of enterprising entrepreneurs. I certainly met a few colourful characters in those rewarding years! Among the beneficial discoveries which I was proud to sponsor was a machine which turned old rags and waste-paper into a very passable imitation of porcelain (this thrilled me to the marrow, as you can imagine) and a most ingenious device to enable deep-sea divers to play chess at depths of up to six hundred feet. Unfortunately, neither of these remarkable innovations was ever taken up by a commercial concern; imagine how the lives of our gallant North Sea oil-workers would have been enriched by the chance of playing underwater chess, and the corresponding increase in productivity that would have followed.

There were of course totally useless inventions, with which I had little patience. I remember one particularly fatuous example, which was claimed to have been invented by an eight-year-old Hungarian child, would you believe! It consisted of a cube made up of about six different colours, the purpose of which entirely escaped me. It was very badly made, too; it was, of course, the product of a socialist country – the colours were all jumbled up – and it was impossible to put them back together again. After my clerk had wasted a whole morning fiddling with the wretched thing I snatched it from him and threw it out of the window.

Most of my briefs (another legal technical term, I hasten to say) were extremely tangled, and tended to be about who had invented what first. In 1953, for example, I was tied up for ages with hula-hoops, and I soon tired of the endless succession of expert witnesses who trooped in to wiggle those infernal devices at me for hours on end. Then there was a woman who claimed to have developed a non-slip plastic material; I was quite interested in her idea, since it related directly to my own work on polymers at Oxford. Regrettably, she tripped over a loose floorboard and injured her neck, and then had the effrontery to bring an action against me under the Defective Premises Act! However, my chemical training came to my aid, and I was able to lodge a counterclaim on the grounds that her so-called invention was directly plagiarised from certain unpublished results of my own and the claim was successfully compromised.

Well, although this work was utterly fascinating, enabling me to thrill dinner-parties with my tales of edible newspapers and see-through bricks, I felt that it was scarcely furthering my political career. So, regretfully, I put the field of patents behind me and turned my attentions to revenue law. Since then, I can safely say, I have never looked back. In fact, it would not be going too far to say that the present taxation structure of this country is a direct result of my days as a revenue lawyer, since it gave me an invaluable insight into the iniquities of the taxation system. Day after day I was faced with heart-rending tales of hard-working men and women who had striven to build up successful businesses – often whole groups of companies, based in such under-developed parts of the British Isles as Alderney and the Isle of Man – only to have the fruits of their labours snatched from them by an insensitive and Communist-inspired tax regime. Thanks to my revenue work, I made the acquaintance of men who were to become the leaders of British industry. You know, I can think of no better example of the rewards of hard work and selfless pursuit of excellence than the way that now, after all these years, many of my old tax clients still spare the time from the pressures of work to give me the benefit of their advice and experience on fiscal matters, particularly in the weeks immediately before the Budget. It only goes to show the wisdom of casting one's bread upon the waters!

So, instead of hula-hoops and plastic cubes, I was dealing with such important and meaningful matters as estate duty exemptions and revenue clearances. I found it immensely enjoyable and fulfilling, and when Father started taking an interest in my work – it seemed that he was mixed up in some sort of ludicrous misunderstanding with his local Inspector of Taxes – my joy was complete. His encyclopaedic knowledge of revenue law and practice came as a complete surprise to me – I had never thought of him as a man who indulged in hobbies – and he often sent me hypothetical problems to solve, until we had a regular fiscal correspondence, just like those people who play chess by post. In particular he seemed interested in a potential loophole in the purchase tax regulations, and I must confess that I would never have spotted it myself. I was so impressed with it that when a client came to me with exactly that problem, I passed it on to him (for it was perfectly legal) and he was so impressed that he offered me a very well-paid job on the spot! Unfortunately, his company was based on an island called Sark, which turned out to be too far from London for me to commute to in comfort, and so I was forced to decline.

Naturally, I never for one moment allowed my work to get in the way of my duties as housewife and homemaker; as I rather wittily put it, if it came to a choice between my briefs being unread or Denis's briefs being unwashed, the washing would have to take priority. There was one wifely duty which gave me more pleasure than almost anything else, and that was washing Denis's rugby strip when he came home after refereeing a match. He was a first-class referee for many years, until an unfortunate injury to his back – caused by a clumsy player pushing him from his bar-stool in the clubhouse after a match – brought an end to his career. Sometimes, as a special treat, he would let me scrub his back for him after I had cleaned his boots, and as he sat contentedly in the tub with a glass of his favourite tonic water in his hand, I would lather and scrub away until I could almost see my reflection in his skin. As Father always used to say, the family that cleans together leans together.

My blossoming career in revenue law was not the only wonderful thing that I remember from the 1950s. The Festival of Britain did much to revitalise hope for the future and, more importantly, the economy. In fact, I do believe the time is right for a similar celebration, and as soon as a suitable pretext can be found – the Silver Jubilee of my accession, for example – I shall order one.

In 1952 the first television sets began to make their appearance in homes all over the country. Now I am sure that I am not alone in regarding the television as a mixed blessing; although it offers a politician like myself un-rivalled opportunities for communicating her message to the people, I fear that most of the broadcasting companies and the whole of the BBC are now so riddled with left-wing subversives who stop at nothing to peddle their obnoxious propaganda to an unwary nation that nothing short of major intervention will set the situation right. Another thing I shall have to deal with soon, I suppose!

Of course, in the innocent days of 1952 all these developments were undreamed of, and I vividly recall the day when our first television set arrived. As I sat and stared in amazement at that flickering screen, little did I realise that I would one day appear on it myself! Soon the proceedings of Parliament will be televised, and thus I shall have a series of my own, which I trust will replace *Neighbours* at the top of the ratings. I have yet to think of an appropriate name for it; my Press Office has made vari-ous suggestions, such as *The Good Life* and *Immortality Knocks*, but I have not yet made a final choice. For his part, Denis does not greatly care for television, except for the sports programmes. His current favourite is snooker, and he tells me that he particularly enjoys watching the end of each frame when the white has finished knocking the reds about and sends the black down a hole.

While we are on the subject of the television, I was

amused to notice in that splendid American drama series *Texas* that shoulderpads and dark red lipstick are once again in fashion, for of course they were very much the 'look' of the 1950s. As I have said before, I have always preferred timeless elegance to the dictates of fashion, with the result that I look much the same now as I did then. But this timelessness did not prevent me from taking an interest in all forms of popular culture, and I managed to snatch a few precious hours from my work to see Joan Crawford in all her most famous films – a woman of tremendous character and sensitivity, I always felt, while her loving family who frequently appeared with her on the television at Christmas struck a chord in my heart – and of course I never missed a new Ronald Reagan picture, come what may. Almost the first thing I said to him when I met him for the first time was to compliment him on his performance as Zeke in *Gunsmoke at Apache Creek*, for me one of the highlights of twentieth-century drama. Typically modest, the President claimed to have forgotten all about it!

The more astute of you will have realised that the 1950s mean so much to me because they saw the second most important event of my life: the birth of my twin children, Carol and Mark. Curiously enough, Joan Crawford is connected with this event in a remote way since I firmly believe that the twins started their journey towards Life, so to speak, on the evening after Denis and I returned from watching *Mildred Pierce* at the Odeon, Leicester Square.

The twins were born at sixteen minutes past six on 14th August 1953 at Queen Charlotte's Hospital in London. They were seven weeks premature, thus continuing the family tradition of enterprise and get-up-and-go, and weighed four pounds each. You may be surprised that I can remember these details after so many years, but they are precisely the sort of thing that a mother never forgets; besides, I can date it precisely by the retail price index, which I read on the way to the hospital.

The births, with two minutes between them, were by caesarian section (as Denis said recently, even then I was in favour of extensive cutting in health matters!) and since I had spent the last few weeks of my pregnancy preparing for my Bar Finals I remember feeling a degree of confusion at being surrounded by white-coated doctors after spending so long in the company of dark-suited lawyers. It is not true, however, that when I first saw Mark I promptly appealed to the House of Lords; that's just another of Denis's witticisms. Denis was not able to attend the birth, as it happened; he was called away at the last minute to witness the final over in the Ashes test match at Lord's.

And now I have a great confession to make. Soon after the births I was so moved that I wrote a poem on the back of my Trusts and Equity lecture-notes (for I did not allow my moment of fulfilment as a woman to interfere with my revision). I would like to share it with you now.

A Mother's Joy

People say a mother's joy
Is always a boy.
But the cost is dear
And paid for with a tear.
Joy must always be paid for;
That's what we were made for
(So never throw something away,
You may need it again some day,
Nor should you yearn
To pay yourself more than you earn)
But I have no regrets that I have striven
And I'm grateful that I was given

A daughter and *a son,*
Two for the price of one;
And, most of all, that I was staunch
At their launch.

Believe me, dear reader, there is a tear in my eye as I write, and I trust there is one in yours.

As anyone who has given birth will tell you, the first person one wishes to see at that precious moment is one's mother. And of course Mrs Beatrice Roberts came down as soon as she heard the news, bringing with her a characteristic gift of some cold dripping and a bag of corduroy offcuts from a waistcoat she had made for Father. As soon as she saw the two infants her eyes filled with tears. 'Oh Margaret,' she exclaimed, 'isn't it true what I've always told you, that God makes little children, even though it's Satan who generally brings them up.' Then, at once, she set to making baby clothes out of the corduroy offcuts and a few worn-out towels that she managed to rescue from the hospital's laundry-room before they were thrown away. It gives me great pleasure to think that Carol and Mark were thus surrounded with the fruits of sensible frugality literally from the moment of their birth.

Inevitably the naming of the twins caused us great concern. I wanted to call them Beatrice and Alfred. My mother, carried away by Coronation fever, suggested Elizabeth and Philip (rather dowdy names, I have always felt) while Denis was all in favour of calling our son Jan Pretorius Thatcher, which he said had a nice ring to it. In the end I compromised on Carol and Mark, and to this day I cannot think what decided me on those names. The only explanation I have been able to come up with is that my mind was full of my Bar Finals in December, and that I called Carol after Christmas and Mark after what I hoped to get plenty of in my Trusts and Equity paper. In the end, though, I think my choice was a good one. Above all I wanted simple names for my children, and that is the way they have turned out.

Only a mother could understand this, but I would have been proud of my children no matter what sort of adults they had grown into; even if Mark had grown up into a feckless playboy or Carol into a featherbrained lightweight, I would still have loved them. I was born to be a mother, and I cherish the memory of those childhood days, when Mark would play with his toy cars on the kitchen floor and Carol (who was always inclined to be something of a tomboy) would snatch a car from his hands and drop it down in the middle of the dessert, where we would have terrible trouble finding it. Carol was always literary, for she kept a diary from an early age, in which she wrote down everything she did and heard. When she was growing up the house was often full of MPs and other luminaries, and several quotations recorded in Carol's diary, which I confess I had completely forgotten, have come in extremely useful since.

Carol has always been an excellent mixer, able to make conversation with anyone from an ambassador to the ordinary men and women at any Conservative conference or Young Conservative dinner, despite a slight speech impediment (not inherited from the Roberts' side of the family, I hasten to add). Mark, however, has always been inclined to be a trifle – how shall I put it? – heavy-handed with his social inferiors; I'm afraid he hasn't inherited my sensitivity and common touch.

It was Carol who followed in my footsteps by going to university and reading law, although she later abandoned the legal profession to follow her love of journalism. At first, as you can imagine, I was rather apprehensive about this. The British press, once the bastion of freedom, is now so saturated with Communism through the pernicious efforts of the NUJ that one feels ashamed to admit that one's daughter is in any way involved with it. However, Carol overcame this obstacle and after a brief flirtation with LSD, as I believe the radio station she worked for was called, she settled down to a job on the *Daily Telegraph*, and my worries were at an end. She also found time to write a book about the marriage of those splendid young tennis players Christopher Evert and Joan Lloyd, shortly before they filed for divorce. As a mother, I cannot resist showing off my daughter's prodigious talent to the world. Here is a short quotation from *Election Diary*, her account of one of my many election victories. It was, I need hardly say, written entirely spontaneously and with no assistance from me:

Friday   Rained. Gosh, didn't Mummy look super and radiantly wondrous this morning and to think that she only had three hours sleep though she looked even nicer on *News at Ten* in that scrummy blue georgette with the little mauve bow which was much nicer than what Michael Foot had on which looked like he'd slept in it for a week in the bath while Shirley Williams hair looked like an owl had nested in it so I don't think anyone will vote for her or not any women at any rate because Caroline who's going out with Aubrey who used to go out with Georgina says she's not going to vote for her even though Aubrey said she should because she'll make the price of gold go zooming up if she gets in and that will be wonderful for his shares in De Beers but Aubrey knows nothing at all about politics all he thinks about is that new Porsche of his with the sticker in the back window that says My Other Car's A Ferrari which is just like him all over and when I think how I cried myself to sleep that time he said my new hairdo made me look like a hanging

basket I could kick myself I really could and everyone said
that Mummy looked miles better than David Dimbleby
too although that's not saying much he was wearing a
lavender tie with a pearl grey suit and Aubrey says that
only proles wear lavender with grey and he should know
because he meets lots of them in the City

One of the first things my children learned, even
before they could walk, was to stand on their own two
feet, and as a result I have never had to worry about either
of them using my position to obtain an unfair advantage
in life. Carol is fortunate in having her God-given talent
for words, but Mark has nothing apart from his determination and a certain flair as an entrepreneur, which he
has of course inherited from his Thatcher ancestors.

To begin with, he started off with a modest management consultancy in Surrey, but the urge to make
something of himself has led him to create his own
opportunities, and I am proud to say that his business
empire now includes such diverse elements as motor-
racing and an interest in a Japanese menswear company.
Like his father, and Father before him, he has never
discussed the details of his business affairs with me –
which is how it should be, needless to say; I belong to a
generation which was brought up to believe that a man's
affairs are his own business. Now, of course, he has
married a charming American girl, and these days I see
very little of him, although Denis meets him whenever
he goes to Las Vegas on business.

The wedding reception took place at the Savoy in
London, which is not the place I would have chosen
myself, since I believe it is one of the ugliest buildings in
the city, and the sooner someone applies for planning
permission to convert it into much-needed office space
the better. However, reasons of security ruled out all the
venues I had chosen, and by and large it was a day I shall

always remember with pleasure. At one point I was nearly in tears, since it brought memories of my own wedding day flooding back: the flowers, the telegrams and the way that Denis insisted on listening to the test match on his portable radio during the ceremony. As it happened, this harmless whim of his nearly caused havoc with the elaborate security arrangements. I believe one of the guards picked up the commentary on his walkie-talkie and was seriously alarmed when he heard that a man with the suspiciously Middle-Eastern-sounding name of Imran Khan had been caught in the covers. My one regret was that I didn't take a larger handbag, since there was a considerable amount of food left over afterwards.

To return, however, to the 1950s. Denis's flat in Swan Court, Chelsea, was ideal for family life. It was easily large enough for our needs – compared to North Parade, Grantham, it was palatial; it took me several months to get used to the idea of an inside loo in my own home – and we seized every opportunity to entertain guests.

We were fortunate in having a well-known theatrical couple, Lewis Casson and Sybil Thorndike, as neighbours. Let me hasten to add that they were married – Mrs Thorndike, as is the custom among actresses, retained her maiden name – so it was a respectable area after all! I have always had a weakness for the theatre, and we got to know the 'dotty duo' (as we affectionately called them) very well. They spoke, of course, in that curious language of the stage that outsiders find difficult to understand at first, and to begin with I was disconcerted when I overheard Mrs Thorndike saying she wished I would break my neck. Later, of course, I learned that this is only a theatrical way of wishing someone good luck. I don't believe they were terribly interested in politics; few actors are, although as usual my friend ex-President Reagan is the glowing exception. In fact they seemed to be interested in very little apart from themselves, and I have often thought how different theatre people are from politicians in that respect. Nevertheless, I have occasionally heard vigorous political comment behind the scenes in Theatreland. I remember the time when I went to see Jeffrey Archer's wonderful drama *Beyond All Reasonable Understanding*. When we went backstage to meet the cast, the stagehands kept shouting 'Hang the blacks!' and 'Kill the workers!' It was all I could do to keep Denis from joining in.

One evening, Mrs Thorndike offered us some tickets for a new comedy which was to open the next week; she was unable to use them herself because of an unforeseen charity dinner. She assured me, however, that the show had been a tremendous success in Paris, where all the best farces came from, and she expected that Denis and I would laugh like anything from beginning to end. The play was called *Waiting for Godot*, and Mrs Thorndike was quite right; Denis and I were in stitches from the moment the curtain went up. If you haven't seen it for yourself I won't spoil the joke for you, but it's a charming little comedy about a couple of drunken dustmen. Oddly enough, Denis and I seemed to be the only ones in the theatre who laughed, and several of the people sitting near us turned and scowled at our merriment. I can only imagine that the comedy went over their heads. Anyway, the purpose of this anecdote is to show what good terms we were on with our glamorous neighbours, and it was with much sadness that we left Swan Court shortly afterwards, when the Labour Government of the day treacherously abolished rent control and the flat became too expensive for us.

We moved to a delightful little house near Farnborough in Kent, which Denis was able to buy thanks to some shrewd investments in Rhodesian mining shares. It was convenient for my work in London, and for a while I busied myself with the pleasures of revenue law and running our home. But the dream of getting into Parliament was never out of my mind for very long, and I continued to look for a constituency. Oxford, Orpington, Beckenham, Ashford, Maidstone and Hemel Hempstead all proved to be unsuitable; but in 1957, I began my long and happy association with Finchley.

To be eligible, the candidate was required to be under forty and to live less than a certain distance from the constituency, but I soon worked out that I met both requirements and took a map with the distances carefully marked on it in red ink and my birth certificate to the selection meeting, where I was adopted with hardly any fuss. A few short years later, a General Election was called.

In my previous elections, I had relied on Father's immense experience of campaigning; but by now he did not feel up to the tremendous effort required, and so Denis consented to take his place. At once he leapt into action, rallying support from the most unexpected quarters. No group of voters was too small for his attention; for example, he took the trouble to canvass a local rugby team, not once but several times, even inviting them home to discuss campaign issues until the early hours of the morning. He must have had a tremendous effect on them, to judge by the enthusiastic laughter that issued from our front room, and he set them to work to learn a campaign song he had written, to the tune of 'Mademoiselle from Armentières'. I felt that the strain of working on my behalf was having a bad effect on his health – he was out canvassing most nights, and invariably had a bad migraine the next day – and once again I was painfully reminded that others, as well as myself, were making great sacrifices so that I could fulfil my destiny.

History, as always, had the last word, and the General Election resulted in a massive Conservative victory. I had a personal majority of over sixteen thousand, and at long last I was a Member of Parliament. Although, through my efforts at self-improvement, I was entitled to write a long string of letters after my name, those two initials 'MP' meant more to me than all the others; indeed, for the first few weeks after the election I even signed the shopping-list and the note for the milkman 'M. Thatcher MP'. Little did I know then, in those heady days of 1959, that within twenty short years I would be in a position to turn them round to read 'PM'.

CHAPTER FIVE

My Burgeoning Destiny

The twentieth of October 1959 probably means little to you unless it happens to be your birthday or wedding anniversary; to me, it is a mixture of both, with even more on top. You see, it was both the beginning of my new life and the marriage of a human being to a mission that would one day eventually be fulfilled. But it was far more than that; it was the day when I finally took my rightful place in the House of Commons as Member of Parliament for Finchley; thus, I cannot help thinking, completing the inexorable movement of history which began with Simon de Montfort and for which men such as Hampden and Pym – John Pym, of course, not Francis Pym – gave their lives.

I shall never forget that day. Sadly, Denis was not able to be with me, since he was in Japan on business; but Father did me the honour of coming all the way from Grantham. He even brought his old friend and solicitor, on the edge of whose desk I had sat when I was a little girl – he told me that they both had to be in London anyway to attend a creditors' meeting, but of course I saw through that flimsy deception at once!

All three of us were naturally impressed with the splendour of the House, which surpassed even Grantham town hall in its stately majesty. It is rightly called a palace – little did I know that one day I was to be its queen! That is, I hasten to add, a figure of speech; I mean no disrespect to Her Majesty, whom I always think of as very much the senior partner in our happy working relationship. For one thing, she is considerably older than I am, and I belong to a generation that was brought up to respect our elders. Father was especially taken with the House of Commons library, and begged me to let him have a few sheets of the notepaper as a souvenir. In fact he was flattering enough to get me to sign a few sheets at the bottom, since the son of a friend of his was a keen collector of autographs. Now, I suppose, those sheets of paper would be quite valuable!

My first day as an MP was rather daunting, but I bore up with all the staunchness at my command. I discovered that the House is chronically short of office space, and that I had been allotted a desk in one of the many corridors. Yet I have always said that there is more honour in a desk in a corridor in the Mother of Parliaments than an office in the biggest and most palatial building outside it, since the corridors of the House are – to coin a phrase – the corridors of Power. I grew very attached to that little desk, tucked away behind the waterpipes, and once I had managed to persuade the cleaning staff to store their brooms and buckets elsewhere, I can honestly say that it was the tidiest and best-polished desk in Westminster. Every morning, before I started my work, I would give it a good going-over with a little beeswax and a scrap of old duster, until I could see my face in it. Now a backbencher by the name of Edward Heath has it; I only hope that he is as happy there as I was, though I don't suppose *he* ever bothers to polish it.

Names such as Macmillan, Selwyn Lloyd, Jenkins, Callaghan, Foot and Healey will mean absolutely nothing to you, I expect; even I have difficulty in putting faces to them after so many years. That is the essence of politics, of course. One lives in the present all the time, and the has-beens and under-achievers of yesteryear are soon forgotten; do *you* remember Ian Gilmour, for example? But in 1959 – you may find this hard to believe – these were the names on everybody's lips, as familiar to the man in the street then as William Waldergrave, John Patten and Douglas Hurd are to the hero-worshipping youngsters of today. Please don't get me wrong; I feel sure that people a hundred years hence will know who Douglas Hurd was, and that his name will be a byword for loyalty and obedience whenever the good old days are talked about!

But perhaps my older readers will understand what I mean when I say what a thrill it was to bump into Aneurin Bevan on one's way to the chamber. Funnily enough, I was always bumping into him and we always laughed as I helped him pick up whatever he happened to be carrying at the time. I even had a nickname for him – 'Nigh' Bevan – because he was always nigh when I turned a corner! He was a fascinating character, and his political success should be a shining example to all immigrants for whom English is not their mother tongue.

In those days the Labour Party was still a force to be reckoned with in British politics, and I seem to remember that their leader was a man called Gaitskell, or Skellgate, or something like that. However, without checking my reference books I cannot be sure, and so I must caution those of my readers who are studying these pages as a 'set book' for their GCSE exams to check in an encyclopaedia. I'm certain it was either Mr Skellgate or Michael Foot; one gets so confused with leaders of the Labour Party, and I have seen too many of them come and go to take much of an interest any more.

Talking of the Labour Party reminds me that in those days there were three different parties at Westminster. The third party was called the Liberal Party – I can't honestly recall what it was all supposed to be about – and one of its longest-serving MPs joined the House on the same day as I did. His name was Jeremy Thorpe, and I remember him particularly because he had a very funny nose. I think he was caught up in some sort of dreadful scandal shortly before his party went into liquidation. Still, every dog must have his day, as the saying goes.

Another of my contemporaries was a woman called Judith Hart, who has now been made a Dame, would you believe! Thankfully, I have never been embarrassed by being offered that title, which always reminds me of pantomime – so appropriate for Miss Hart, of course. She too has faded into obscurity, but in those early days Judith and I were almost friendly since we had in common the strange experience of being women in Parliament. I have always regretted the fact that so few women have been suitable to be MPs but the fact remains that only a handful of women have been able to draw on the sort of support from their husband and family that I have been blessed with. Without that kind of support a woman would not be able to take any part in public life other than by neglecting her duty to her home. While I am on the subject, I would just like to make it clear that I can never condone the idea that a woman is free to neglect her responsibilities for the sake of her career. Let me say that I have *never* burnt my bra like those dreadful left-wing actresses Jane Fonda, Vanessa Redgrave and Joyce Grenfell – they're far too expensive, even if one buys in bulk as I do. On the other hand, I always have opposed, and always will oppose, discrimination on the grounds of gender as much as the next man.

The House of Commons has been called a 'talking shop'; what nonsense! For a start, it's virtually impossible to buy anything there except for a few souvenirs in the lobby, and unlike most shops these days it stays open until the early hours of the morning. Not that there is anything wrong with being like a shop, of course, but we should always remember that the House of Commons, together with 10 Downing Street, is the place where the law of the land is made and the future of the nation is decided. Now the rule of the House (and what a good rule it is too!) makes it virtually impossible for ordinary backbenchers to interfere much with the shaping of legislation, but there is the charming old custom of the Private Member's Bill. When I first heard about the notion in my early days as an MP I thought it was something to do with the purchase of pornographic literature, but Denis soon put me right on that point, and as soon as I realised that I might be fortunate enough to win the ballot I set to thinking of a really useful piece of law that I could sponsor.

I cannot begin to describe the excitement I felt when I found that I had come second in the ballot and that my chance had arrived. For those of you who are working-class, I suppose that a suitable comparison would be cashing in on the pools or winning at bingo in *The Times*. Imagine my dismay, then, when I realised that, at such short notice, I had nothing concrete to propose. Undaunted, I looked around me for a suitable topic. At once, my fertile brain seethed with possibilities. For instance, my work with ice-cream led me to consider a Gelatine (Consolidation) Act. Father chipped in with a well-thought-out proposal about Sunday trading, by which only proven Methodists should be permitted to open their doors on Sundays. The logic behind this was that Methodists, being assured of the Kingdom of Heaven, don't need the luxury of a day devoted entirely to religious contemplation, and of course it makes a great deal of sense. Sadly the administrative provisions that would have been necessary for Father's scheme were too complicated for me to work out in the short time available, and so I was reluctantly forced to shelve the idea until I came to power. In fact, I think there's a committee of civil servants still beavering away at it to this day!

Undaunted, Father went away and came back with a suggestion for an Act to legalise insider dealing; but I felt that the rules of bridge, however seriously some people take the game, aren't really a suitable subject for Parliament. Meanwhile, Denis was working hard too, and came up with a measure to combat the growing menace of spiked shoes on golf courses, which threatened the very grass of our green and pleasant land. I had got as far as the fifth draft of this when I remembered that I had bought Denis a pair of spiked golf shoes for his birthday, and that it was now too late to take them back and claim a refund. Obviously I didn't want to see my own husband thrown into prison, and so the bill had to be scrapped. So in the end I was forced to rely on my own instincts. There was one problem of the day – unfortunately still with us – which I desperately wanted to do something about, and that was the issue of dangerous stationery. At that time I did most of my own paperwork, and I often found that when I licked an envelope the edge of the paper would cut my tongue. At once I set to work on the Paper Sharpness (Especially On One's Tongue) Abolition Act. I spent many a happy hour in the House of Commons library reading the subject up. My researches took me back as far as 1215 – it is a little-known fact that King John cut his hand on the parchment of Magna Carta – and I was on the point of pursuing the topic back into the Dark Ages when I heard from the Whips Office that another problem, equally important and rather more pressing, required to be dealt with.

To my horror, I was informed that two years before, certain Labour councils had supported strikers in the newspaper industry by refusing strike-breakers entry to council meetings. You must remember that this was many years before Rupert Murdoch's crusade to save

Fleet Street, and that industrial action by the press unions was then perfectly legal. As if they needed any encouragement to do nothing! In my experience, nearly all journalists are extremely lazy people who seem to spend all their time lying in the sun. Obviously anything I could do to assist those brave souls who wanted to make a stand against socialist oppression counted for more than my own private causes, and so I resolved to introduce a measure to make press admission to local council meetings a legal right.

I was fortunate enough to find a sponsor in the great W. F. Deedes, then MP for Ashford and familiar to countless millions as a regular contributor to the Peterborough column in the *Daily Telegraph*. According to dear Bill my proposal was 'of Front Bench quality', and I screwed up my courage for my maiden speech. I have been screwing it up ever since, of course, but that first address to the House will live with me to the day I die. It was a short speech – barely three-quarters of an hour – and I spoke without notes. Now that I come to think of it, it was also remarkable for the fact that it was a maiden speech introducing a piece of legislation. As Denis puts it, my word has always been law in the House of Commons.

It was a Friday, I remember, and on Fridays the House is often quite empty, since MPs with remote constituencies in Northamptonshire and Leicestershire tend to leave early. However, the news that I was to speak quickly spread, and there were nearly twenty members assembled to hear me open my mouth for the first time in the House of Commons. Of course they were enchanted at my debut, many of them sitting rooted to the spot and closing their eyes, just as music buffs do at concerts! A word of advice I would give to all aspiring politicians is to get the maiden out of the way as quickly as possible. For example, there is one MP who entered the House at the same time as I did who has yet to make his maiden speech. I expect it will be terribly good when he finally gets round to it.

To return to what I was saying; I could tell almost as soon as I started speaking that I had found my true medium. The words came tumbling out without the need for any thought – I never think before I speak, it impedes the flow – and before I knew where I was the speech was over. My only regret was that I wasn't able to listen to it myself. Nor, unfortunately, was Denis; he had to be in Australia on business.

I soon became as much at home in the House as I was in my kitchen or behind the counter of the little shop in North Parade, Grantham. Of course, there was a lot to learn; the House has hundreds of quaint little traditions which one has to know for fear of making some terrible blunder. For example, it is quite out of order for an MP to shake hands within the confines of the House, a custom which originates from the principle that MPs should not be seen to be doing devious deals. Some politicians have never managed to get used to it after countless years at ·Westminster – there was one venerable old gentleman called John Stonehouse, a one-time member of the Labour Party, whose hand continually wobbled about as he offered it to people and then was suddenly snatched back as he remembered where he was! I remember seeing him meeting some businessmen from his constituency (all wearing raincoats for some reason), and I fancy they were aware of his tendency to breach Parliamentary etiquette, for as soon as he instinctively reached out his hand towards them they each thrust an envelope into it, presumably to avoid the fatal handshake.

For anyone interested in economic history, the 1960s were a thrilling time. I remember the 1961 Budget debate with great clarity. A man called Selwyn Lloyd was

Chancellor of the Exchequer, and I spoke up against the fact that Britain still had the highest rate of tax on working wives of any country in Europe – and I should know, as I told him! You see, my abiding fascination with matters fiscal, acquired during my days at the Bar, was still with me; it was one of the political topics that Denis was most keenly interested in, then as now. In fact, I don't think I'm giving too much away to say that Denis has more than once helped me with knottier points of tax legislation, and I have found his advice invaluable. Unfortunately, he lacks the ability to concentrate, and although his suggestions are invariably useful, he always tends to overlook some silly little loophole that would end up as a tax-dodger's charter.

It was my love of revenue law that first turned my attention to the study of economics. At first I found the whole thing quite baffling. If interest rates are high, this affects the pound. If the pound is high, this affects the trade deficit. If this results in a balance-of-trade problem, it can have an effect on inflation, which in turn has something to do with pay rises, which are thought to be linked to unemployment. I was on the point of giving up when I happened one day to be browsing in a second-hand bookshop, and hidden away among the recipe books I found a volume which has been my bible ever since.

Although the author is not widely known as an economist – his name, apparently, is Ladybird and he seems to have written books about all sorts of things – I cannot recommend his slim volume too highly. Do be sure to look out for it; it's a pleasing yellow colour and quite short, and there are many excellent pictures.

Professor Ladybird explains economic theory in terms of a small grocer's shop. For example, if the grocer has to borrow from the bank to buy the tea and coffee and marmalade he sells, he has to increase the price of things, just as Father did when I went to Oxford. This means that in order for the poor people to be able to buy marmalade, they have to ask their employer for increased wages. As a result their employer has to charge more for the goods he makes; and if he makes marmalade, then the grocer who buys it from him has to charge even more for the same marmalade in the shop, and this can lead to inflation. Fortunately, it rarely happens since a very small percentage of the population are employed in the marmalade industry. However, if the grocer buys a pot of marmalade from France, this means that money leaves the country and won't come back again unless a British marmalade manufacturer sells a pot of marmalade to a French grocer (or *boulanger*, as I believe they're called). Again, this is not a major problem, as French marmalade is so disgusting that nobody could possibly prefer it to the home-produced product. However, if things do get out of hand, the solution is simple. All the grocer has to do is dismiss his assistant and get his daughter to work longer hours in the shop. This saves the assistant's wages, and the grocer needn't put prices up again until it's time for his daughter to go to college. And that's all there is to it. Incidentally, if you ever do come across Professor Ladybird's book (now sadly out of print) at a bring-and-buy sale somewhere, perhaps you might spare a thought for poor Nigel Lawson, who's never been able to get hold of a copy. I would willingly lend him mine, but he's terrible about borrowing things and then forgetting to give them back.

It was not long after I had finally mastered the intricacies of economic theory that the next startling movement in my career overtook me. I remember that I had arranged to meet my sister Muriel for lunch at a place called Claridge's. Just before I set off I received a message from Downing Street asking me to meet the Prime Minister, Harold Macmillan, at Admiralty House. At first I was perplexed by this as I knew next to nothing about sailing, but I rushed off nevertheless. All I could think of was that he wanted me to appear in a Party Political Broadcast or something of the sort.

History always has the last word. I left that meeting with the Old Fool (as we affectionately called him) having been appointed Joint Parliamentary Secretary to the Minister of Pensions and National Insurance. At the time, I don't think I fully appreciated the nature of the appointment, since I remember stopping off on my way home to buy a couple of spiral-backed notepads and a book on shorthand. But as soon as Denis had explained it to me, I hurtled back to my desk to begin work as a Minister. Unfortunately, everyone except the cleaner had gone home by then, but I was too excited to sleep and I was ready at my desk when the doors opened next day. Incidentally, in my excitement I clean forgot all about poor Muriel; for all I know, she's still at Claridge's to this very day! I do hope she hasn't eaten too many éclairs.

I soon found myself at the despatch box answering questions about pensions. I even drafted a speech to make to the Party Conference that year. It was a very good speech and here is an extract from it which I have never been able to fit in anywhere else:

> Pensioners must learn to save their pennies for a rainy day. Certainly for a cold day; the Government can't afford to pay their electricity bill. My father taught me the value of saving. Every Friday night he would take me and my sister down to the cellar, and there we would put the sixpence we had earned behind the counter during the week into a little metal box with a slot while we turned a little handle. It was only when I went to Oxford that I

learned that this was an electricity meter, and thanks to that early lesson I know the value of saving and that electricity has to be paid for. It's that sort of self-reliance that we need to encourage among the old folk of today.

Unfortunately I couldn't deliver the speech, as only senior Cabinet Ministers make policy statements to Conference. However, my time was to come eventually, and I don't suppose anyone who heard it will forget my first speech to the Party in a hurry. It was quite short – little more than two and a half hours – but into that brief time I was able to compress everything I knew about relative pension incomes from 1946 onwards. I compared these incomes with those of old people in other similar countries – Chad, Paraguay, Thailand – and was able to show that the Conservative Government of the day had a better record on pensions than any British government before the Napoleonic War. I enjoyed the first of my countless standing ovations, and my only regret was that Denis wasn't there to hear me. Unfortunately, he was called away to Pietermaritzburg on business shortly before the conference opened.

During my time at the Department of Pensions I saw several Ministers come and go. It was fascinating to sit in on policy meetings and see how the so-called civil servants changed their advice to suit the man in charge. I soon came to realise that the Civil Service never offers advice which it thinks the Minister will reject, and after a while the advice becomes rather limited in scope. All I can say is that any servant of mine had better be extremely civil if he values his job!

Let me give you an example. Within hours of becoming Prime Minister I summoned all the senior civil servants in Whitehall to a meeting. Just for fun, I kept them waiting for half an hour while I made Denis's supper, and told the ushers to set out one less chair than necessary. Then, when I came in, before I so much as sat down and kicked my shoes off I fixed the fattest man there with my eye and said, 'I suppose *you* work in Administration.' Of course he just sat there and stared. 'Hands up all of you who work in Administration,' I said. None of them moved a muscle. 'I don't suppose you even know how many of you work in Administration,' I went on. 'Well, I'll tell you. It's about *one* in *four*.'

That soon wiped any semblance of a smile off their faces, as you can imagine.

Oh, if only it was as easy to get rid of bureaucrats as it is to dismiss one's Cabinet colleagues! I once asked someone why the Ministers as a collective body were called the Cabinet and I was told that a cabinet is a hollow object made up of dead wood. People think that I was not the first Prime Minister to understand the importance of keeping a balanced, well-rationalised Cabinet, and point to Macmillan's so-called Night of the Long Knives as an example. I always tell them that on that occasion nearly half the Cabinet remained totally unchanged.

Of course, there's more to managing a Cabinet than simply sacking people. If I may put it this way, one shouldn't butcher one's Cabinet so much as carve slices off it, like the Sunday roast, a bit at a time. I even take the trouble to warn a Cabinet colleague of his impending disgrace by sending him an appropriate present, such as a jar of mint sauce or a few bayleaves. Sometimes the poor things mistake this for a friendly gesture, and their delightful thank-you letters have often crossed in the post with their letters of dismissal. Here are a few which always amuse me when I read them:

NORMAN St JOHN-STEVAS

The fourth day of January,
One Thousand Nine Hundred
and Eighty One (St Barnabas the
Lesser and St Galahantine of
Utrecht)

My dear, dear Margaret—

How can I ever find words to thank you for your gift of Marks and
Spencer horseradish — so small a jar, holding so much! It chances that
I have never sampled this *particular* brand, since my narrow horizons
are bounded by Fortnum on the one hand and Mason on the other.
However, I'm having a little dinner-party for Ned, Antonia, Harold,
Bernard and of course dear, dear Germaine; and so positive am I that
this little *bijou* of a jar will keep us enthralled all evening that I'm putting
it centre table. I have a little seventeenth-century Milanese silver dish
that matches its rather adventurous colour scheme perfectly.

Yours, as ever,

Norman

1O DOWNING STREET
LONDON SW1A 2AA
THE PRIME MINISTER

Dear Norman,

Fooled you! You're fired.

Yours ever,

Margaret

DEPARTMENT OF EMPLOYMENT

14th August 1981

Dear Margaret,

Thank you for the jar of pickled walnuts.
I've given them to my chauffeur.

For the last time, I will **not** go to
Northern Ireland. Not now, not next year,
never. This is my final word on the
subject.

Yours sincerely,

James Prior

10 DOWNING STREET
LONDON SW1A 2AA
THE PRIME MINISTER

Dear Mr Prior,

You'll go to Northern Ireland and like
it.

Yours ever,

Margaret Thatcher (Mrs)

THE FOREIGN OFFICE
No job too big or too small
Written quotations on request

Dear Margaret,

Thank you so much for the jellied eels.

 Congratulations on yet another victory.
We all knew you had it in you. You keep
sailing blithely on, just like the
Belgrano. God bless you and all who sail
with you!

Your friend,

Francis Pym

10 DOWNING STREET
LONDON SW1A 2AA
THE PRIME MINISTER

Dear Francis Pym,

On your bike.

Yours ever,

Margaret Thatcher (Mrs)

At the moment I believe I have a very strong Cabinet – but I'm sure that this is not an insuperable problem. Obviously, I don't know all their names yet – it hardly seems worth the effort when you think that in a few months most of them will have moved on or returned to where they came from – but although there are some whom I genuinely admire I find Cabinet Government is an overrated institution. I was reminded of this recently when some ill-mannered lout on the Labour benches launched into an endless tirade about the so-called plight of the unemployed. 'Look,' I said to him, 'the unemployed only have to put up with mindless boredom and despair; I have to work with John Selwyn Gummer!'

As you can see, a sense of humour is an invaluable attribute of a Prime Minister, and I always like to break the ice at Cabinet meetings with a little joke. My favourite, which usually goes down well, is this:

'I have decided to spread more light on the workings of Cabinet. Nigel, stand away from the window at once!'

That's so funny, isn't it?

Talking of Cabinet Ministers, I cannot help mentioning the rather sad business that shook us all in 1963, just when I was getting into my stride as a Minister. People nowadays call it the Profumo 'scandal', although I always feel that that is rather an exaggeration. It's all ancient history now, of course, and even at the time it was never exactly clear what happened. But since you've probably never even heard of it, I had better explain it briefly to you now.

John Profumo, a Minister at the War Office, belonged to some association (it was a choir or a bridge club or something of the sort) of which a lady by the name of Christine Keeler was a member. Miss Keeler also belonged to another association, another bridge club or whatever, which included someone who worked at the Russian Embassy. As you can see, the whole thing was entirely innocent, and had nobody taken it upon themselves to interfere no doubt Mr Profumo and Miss Keeler and the Russian gentleman would all still be happily singing away or playing bridge, or doing whatever it was they did, to this day. Unfortunately, the gutter press got hold of the story, and Mr Profumo was soon so muddled that he made a mistake in a statement to the House about the matter. I can't remember what it was – perhaps he said the association was a whist drive when it was a bridge club, or something of the sort – and when this was pointed out to him he felt so ashamed of having made a muddle that he felt obliged to resign. This put so much pressure on the Prime Minister of the day, Harold Macmillan, that his health was affected and he resigned too. Lord Home of the Hirsel made the ultimate sacrifice and renounced his title to take over as Prime Minister on 10th October 1963 and so everything ended happily after all.

All this came flooding back to me when I saw another glittering career in danger of being ruined by foolish scandal. On the night of one of my numerous General Election victories (this one was in 1983) Cecil Parkinson whispered something in my ear as I stood on the balcony acknowledging the cheers and shouts of 'Ten more decades!' I didn't catch exactly what he said because of the cheering, but it seemed to me that the poor man was worried that he was pregnant!

Now as I have already told you I am a scientist by training, and so I knew that this was impossible. However, I didn't want to upset him, so I tried to explain matters gently. I said that pregnancy tests were notoriously unreliable and that unless he had been feeling sick in the mornings or craving for banana-and-mustard sandwiches, there was probably nothing to worry about.

This only seemed to make him worse, and finally I grasped what he was trying to say. He explained that *he* wasn't pregnant, but that his secretary was. He seemed terribly upset about this, and I can sympathise; a politician relies so much on a loyal and capable assistant, and it can take years to train a girl to set a letter out properly and file things away where you can find them. I sympathised, of course, but poor Cecil seemed to take it very much to heart. He seemed to feel that without the help of this secretary he would be unable to discharge his duties properly. I had always known that he was a perfectionist and took a particular pride in his correspondence, but for the life of me I couldn't see why he felt he had to give up his ministerial post. I even offered to buy him a word processor to tide him over until his girl was back at work again, but he didn't seem to take any notice. So, reluctantly, I was forced to accept his resignation.

To make matters worse, the press immediately started the most appalling smear campaign against him, accusing him among other things of adultery. I was greatly relieved that I knew the true facts of the matter, since adultery is one of the seven deadly sins, and I could not for the life of me understand why Cecil never told the true story to the newspapers. I can only imagine that, like the truly chivalrous man he is, he wanted to protect his secretary from the attentions of reporters during her confinement. Anyway, this story also has a happy ending, since Cecil is now once again a member of the Cabinet. I imagine that his secretary must have had her baby and gone back to work for him again. Certainly, his letters are as well typed as ever.

In October 1964 the Labour Party won a General Election and were temporarily in power until 1970. In spite of this, life went on, and I was at least able to spend a little more time with my family. After the tension of high office the mundane daily routine of an ordinary housewife was something of a relief to me, and I was able to enjoy some of the simple pleasures of life that politics had denied me: the pleasure of a modest family holiday at Lenzerheid, the joyful reunion when Mark came home from boarding school or the celebrations when Denis announced that he had been elected to the board of yet another major company. There was also a great family occasion when Father married his second wife (I should mention that my mother died in 1960; and although I don't feel the slightest bitterness about it, I cannot help wondering why she chose to leave most of her recipe books and her best shoes to Muriel instead of me).

Father's new bride was a very suitable lady by the name of Cissie, who had been widowed several years before. I am honestly able to say that Father would have remained true to my mother's memory, despite the fact that in her last years her character had sadly changed for the worse – towards the end it was not unusual for her to fritter away a shilling a week on buttons – had it not been for sound motives of economy and frugality. Quite unconsciously, while working in the Ministry of Pensions, I had introduced regulations which made it far more economical for pensioners to marry than to live singly. I had been alarmed at the number of old people who were driven to live in sin by economic pressures, and it was characteristic of Father that when he saw a way in which he could not only save money himself but help another human being to do the same, he did not hesitate. I was so pleased for them both that I went to the wedding, although Denis was prevented from joining me by business commitments in Brazil. It was a quiet ceremony, and well worth the admission fee.

So, the nineteen-sixties were very much a decade of domestic happiness for me. Since I took my duties as wife and mother very much to heart, I accumulated a wealth of useful household tips which I would like to share with you now.

Something that any young couple setting up home together for the first time should take particular care over is buying furniture. Unless it is British-made, new furniture is rarely worth the money as it is quite likely to be shoddily put together. One is far better advised to buy good second-hand furniture and make loose covers for it as and when necessary. This also enables you to find a use for any old pieces of material that you happen to have put by. Always buy a deep-seated sofa with soft cushions, and when guests come to call, insist that they sit in it. You will be amazed to find how much small change accumulates under the cushions in a relatively short time – so much that a really soft sofa will pay for itself in a few years. I have a splendid example at Number Ten, from which I have retrieved a small fortune; not only in British currency but in marks, dollars, francs, pesetas and even roubles. Whenever Geoffrey Howe calls, I can be sure of at least a pound.

Clothes can also be a nightmare unless one uses one's common sense. *Always* bulk-buy underwear; it's the only way. I find that unless I know that I have at least five sets of everything I can't rest easily at nights. Of course it would be wrong of me to recommend any one retailer, but I must point out that C & A is foreign while S & M is a truly British institution. One should always carry at least one spare pair of tights in one's handbag. This simple precaution has saved me the embarrassment of arriving at economic summits with ladders. Another essential for one's handbag is a pair of gloves – one never knows who one may have to shake hands with, particularly in politics.

Of course, it's no good looking wonderful oneself if one's husband lets one down. I have always taken the precaution of choosing Denis's clothes for him; on the occasions when he hasn't been available, I find someone of the same size and take him (for the last twenty years,

I've made do with Nicholas Ridley). Although Denis has never been a problem in this respect, I cannot say the same about my Cabinet colleagues. In fact, I think it would be a good idea to institute a uniform for Cabinet, along the lines of those smart outfits that the staff in hotels and building societies wear. I haven't had time to give it much thought, but I envisage a simple charcoal-grey suit with an MT insignia on the breast pocket.

Scruffiness is one thing; frugality is another. You should never ever throw anything away if you can conceivably find a use for it. Although I pride myself on my economy, I must admit that Barbara Bush, the wife of the American President, has taken further steps. She's worked out exactly what to do with old clothes. She wears them.

For the working woman, cooking can be a millstone round the neck. I have solved this problem by putting together a few nourishing but simple and inexpensive recipes and sticking to them. The best example of these is Cabinet Pudding. When I first found the recipe I was so thrilled with it that I made nothing else for six months! The perfect Cabinet Pudding is made entirely from stale crusts and leftovers, and it has long been a favourite at 10 Downing Street. At home I have a secret codeword for Cabinet Pudding – I call it a 'Kenneth Clarke' – and so used am I to that nickname that I sometimes forget that everyone else isn't in on the secret. I remember one occasion when we entertained an African Head of State *en famille* at Chequers. I was just giving the final instructions to the cook and told her to put 'Kenneth Clarke' in the oven and turn the gas up. My guest must have overheard me, since he said that they had a similar way of dealing with superfluous politicians in his country! I assume you all have the recipe for this marvellous dish, but I would like to recommend one tip to you; never let the mixture get too moist. A wet Cabinet Pudding is no use to anyone.

In 1988 there was a lot of fuss and nonsense about eggs. Of course, I took no notice, and insisted on my boiled egg with three soldiers in bed on Sunday morning, come what may. My mother would have laughed to hear today's so-called experts saying that this and that was bad for you; when I was young we were grateful to get any food at all! I particularly remember how Father used to make a point of bringing home any dead rabbits he found run over in the road; my mother always managed to make a tasty meal out of them, and there was the additional bonus of a few coppers for the skin. On one occasion he even managed to bring home a dead sheep, and we had hours of fun paunching it and combing out the wool. Today's housewife probably wouldn't have the faintest idea of what to do with a dead sheep. I mentioned this to Denis once, and he replied that most women could make something out of a dead sheep, but only I could make one Foreign Secretary!

Much as I have enjoyed this digression – like all women, I love nothing better than talking about household things – I must get back to my story. My first moment of true power was just around the corner, and the gates of a new horizon were about to unfold themselves before me. But from the domestic advice I have offered, you can see that I have never allowed my career to distract me from hearth and home. In fact, one of these days I think I will have to find time to sit down and write out all the tips and recipes that I have gathered together. I feel that a collection of that sort would be far more use to the poor families of Britain than all the job creation schemes and youth opportunities programmes in the world.

CHAPTER SIX

By the Grace of God

In 1970 the nightmare lapse into socialism was over and a Conservative government was rightfully back in charge of the country. Doubtless ordinary people everywhere breathed a sigh of relief that the nineteen-sixties were over! For some reason it has come to be known as the Swinging Sixties, a nickname which has always puzzled me since hanging was abolished quite some time earlier but in any event, there can have been few right-thinking people who were sorry to see the back of that troubled time.

The leader of the Party then was a funny little man by the name of Edward Heath. You may recall that he was the man who eventually inherited my desk in the corridor of the House, and that is probably how history will best remember him; he inherited my desk, and I inherited his. However, strange as it may seem, this awkward and basically untalented man was for a brief spell the Prime Minister of Great Britain!

His ineptitude can best be illustrated by a little story which concerns him and Enoch Powell, a man I have always respected despite his left-wing views. Curiously enough, Enoch Powell is one of the few under-achievers in the Conservative Party who has actually gone to Northern Ireland of his own free will! At the time, however, he was still more or less an orthodox Conservative, and he happened to make a speech in an obscure little town in the north called Birmingham in which he quoted some classical text (a habit he was still greatly addicted to) about the streets of Rome, or Troy, I forget which, running with rivers of blood. I don't suppose anybody remembers that speech now, but I happened to come across it in one of my old scrapbooks the other day and it struck me as a totally uncontroversial, almost bland, little effort. But poor Mr Heath – 'Ted' as he was affectionately known, since he reminded everybody of a rather worn-out teddy bear with the stuffing coming out of the seams – took it upon himself to say that Mr Powell had got the quotation wrong, and that it should have been something like 'the bloody streets of Venice are like rivers'. In fact, I remember that there was quite a lot of fuss and nonsense in the newspapers about that speech in the end. I mean, who cares whether the quotation was right or not? The upshot of it all was that Enoch has spent the last twenty years trying to prove that his rendering was the right one – and my knowledge of Latin tells me that what Enoch said in 1968 was pretty close to the truth. But I digress.

In fact, Ted was always getting himself caught up in silly little entanglements like that, and he generally came out of them looking ridiculous. Another example is the idiotic nickname that he was given by Harold Wilson, who was the leader of the socialists at that time – younger readers will probably know him as the raincoat man. The background to all this was that the Tory Shadow Cabinet held a meeting at a place called Selsdon Park to discuss policies and things, and the next day Harold Wilson started talking about a curious entity called 'Selsdon Man'. I think it was supposed to be some sort of joke about the Missing Link and Neolithic Man – it went right over the heads of most MPs, I remember, and I had to explain it to several of my colleagues – but Ted took it all desperately seriously. Admittedly, he does look the part

– it must be the way his jaw seems to disappear into his neck – but in fact he's younger than Harold Wilson, and so there's really very little point in it at all. But then, Harold always did have a most peculiar sense of humour, as his working relationship with Marcia Falkender made all too clear.

The reason why I'm boring you with these silly little tales is to show two things: first, that poor Ted wasn't terribly popular even with his own Party (something that could never be said of me); second, that Harold Wilson was too sure of himself by half. When he called a General Election in 1970 he actually believed that he could win! But of course the cocky little man was sent packing by the staunch British electorate, which goes to prove the truth of the old saying that in a democracy, people tend to get the government they deserve.

Predictably, Ted made a dreadful muddle of choosing his Cabinet. In fact, I am told that for a long time he thought the Cabinet was where the drinks were kept, and his idea of a Cabinet reshuffle was three parts gin to one part vermouth. As a result, people weren't terribly keen to take places in his Government. One man called Sir Edward Boyle had been grooming himself throughout our spell in Opposition to take over Education; but when the time came he left education entirely and took a job in a university.

Poor Ted was stuck but I saw this as my cue to come to the rescue. I knew it would be useless to try and explain to him why I was ideally suited for the post, so one morning bright and early I went to Number Ten and waited about in the hall until his secretary took in his morning cup of tea and jam doughnut. As soon as the secretary came out again I went straight in and told Ted that I was going to be his Minister of Education. Since his mouth was full of doughnut he was unable to say anything, and by the time he had finished chewing I was halfway to Curzon Street.

As you can imagine, everyone there was overjoyed when I told them the good news.

I have already told you something about the nature of civil servants. The prospect of trying to deal with a notoriously obstructive, lazy, secretive and feckless staff daunted me at first, but I sensibly asked Denis for his advice and he said that, basically, civil servant is just a fancy name for employee, and that if I treated them like he treated his employees they would soon be far too worried about losing their jobs to get up to any sort of silly nonsense. I don't think Denis meant this quite literally; for example, all Denis's South African employees have special villages built for them to live in and get free transport to work in company buses. I wouldn't countenance that sort of mollycoddling in a Government department!

Encouraged by Denis's good advice, I sent for my Permanent Secretary at once. From the start I encouraged him to think positively and to follow my orders implicitly. In order to clarify this concept I reduced it to just one sentence; and since it was the Ministry of Education, I thought it would be appropriate if he repeated it after me (which he did). Just to make sure, I made him write out 'I must do what I am told' fifty times that evening.

During my time at the Department of Education there was a continuing debate about so-called comprehensive education. The more time I spend in politics, the more I believe that things are given names that mean the opposite of what they say. For example, the Home Secretary never types a letter from one year's end to the next, the Department of Health is meant to help the sick, not the healthy, and the Foreign Secretary is invariably English. On this principle, comprehensive education is so called because it is totally incomprehensible.

I did my best to prevent comprehensive schools, God knows, but the damage had already been done by the

Labour Party, and all I could do was try and salvage something from the wreck. Unfortunately, I was too late to prevent the abolition of the eleven-plus, and that act of wanton vandalism was allowed to go through, with results that can be plainly seen in magistrates' courts all over the country to this day. I defy anyone to say that if the eleven-plus was still in existence we would have any of this trouble with mindless hooliganism among our young people. Instead we would have a younger generation we could be proud of, all of them able to spell 'separate' and tell you instantly where Istanbul is, or who won the Battle of Tinchebrai.

It was also my misfortune to witness the destruction of grammar schools. To this day I often have nightmares, in which Carol and Mark come home with their satchels over their shoulders and tell me that their school is to become a comprehensive in a week's time and that they will start inviting their schoolfriends home for tea. It was that, I think, which resolved me to give every school the choice to opt out of local government control. I firmly believe, and always will, that everyone should have a choice, just so long as it's a choice between suitable alternatives. That way, perhaps, we can get our educational system back to what it was in my day, or even in Father's.

No sooner had I got the Ministry shipshape than the Chancellor, a man called Anthony Barber, told everyone that he wanted spending cuts in every area of Government. You would have thought that with a name like Barber he would be used to sensible cutting, but let me tell you, I wouldn't let him cut my toenails, let alone my hair! Obviously, it is the prime duty of any Government, second only to the defence of the Falklands, to cut public spending to the bone. But, as I pointed out at the time, my Department – naturally – was a model of efficiency, and there was no room for any more cutting, since I had done it all myself. The thought that someone else was to tell me what to cut and when to cut it struck me as outrageously unfair. What sort of a country would this be, I asked myself, if I am not to be permitted to cut my own Department how I like, when I like?

Cutting is a science – I might almost say an art. If you rush in and chop away at the first thing you see, you might very well find that you have made it impossible for yourself to cut the really important things later on, and then where would you be? As I always say, if you can restrain yourself from cutting nurses today, you'll be able to cut hospitals tomorrow. And there's no better illustration of this than my own experience at Education. Barber wanted me to cut the Open University – if you've never heard of it, it's a sort of correspondence school originally set up so that people in prison could learn sociology to find out what made them into criminals in the first place – but I wasn't having any of that, I can tell you. At the time, it was a tiny little operation employing only a handful of staff in modest little premises, and nobody seemed aware of its very existence. What on earth would have been the point of cutting *that*?

Immediately, I explained to the Home Secretary that the Open University saved the prison service millions of pounds a year by giving the authorities an excuse to lock the criminals up in their cells for hours on end with their textbooks. I then explained to the Employment Minister that if prisoners stopped studying they would have to be given work to do, making mailbags and digging ditches, and that would mean less jobs for the lower classes and immigrants, which in turn would mean higher unemployment. As a result of my logical arguments, the Open University was saved for another day. Now, of course, it's a household name with hundreds of staff, a great big office in Milton Keynes and its own pension scheme, and thus an obvious candidate for closure.

Having avoided the monstrous error of judgement that Barber wanted to foist on to me, I was able to get down to actually achieving something. I had already decided, within hours of setting foot in Curzon Street, what I was going to cut. Ever since my schooldays, I had worried about the scandal of free school milk, and a chance encounter with a common milkman finally resolved me to put my wishy-washy liberal ideas behind me and grasp the nettle.

I remember that one morning I had indulged myself to the point of lazing in bed until well after a quarter to six, and that I was just yawning and putting on my dressing-gown before settling down to my first red box of the day when I heard that characteristically British sound, the grating of milk bottles on the front step a door or so down the street. I remembered that it was Thursday, which in our little family home at Flood Street always meant tapioca pudding, and so I would need an extra pint. I scrambled into my clothes – I would never dream of talking to tradesmen in my dressing-gown – pulled a comb through my hair and rushed out to catch the milkman.

The honest fellow recognised me at once – I can't think how, for in my dishevelled state I must have looked like Shirley Williams in a Party Political Broadcast – and remarked that he had seen me on the television the previous evening. I couldn't grasp everything he said because of his accent (he explained that he came from a town called Cockney, which I believe is somewhere in Hertfordshire) but I could grasp enough of it to understand that he was trying in his humble way to make a policy suggestion. Now I have always made it a rule of my life to listen to everyone, even my Cabinet, and what that milkman said made a great deal of sense! I can remember his very words to this day.

''Ere's an 'onest enterprernoor like meself,' he said,

'strugglin' to make an 'onest bob or two, an' get an 'onest day's pay for an 'onest day's work, like, tha knows, sellin' me bit o' milk like, and there be you pollytishens up to the 'Ouses of Parlyment a-givin' the stuff away to they kiddies in t'schools, by Gow, me old pal, me old beauty. It's enough ter make yer weep, begorrah, innit?'

At once, my mind darted back to that fateful day in Grantham when I had dropped the milk bottle, and my days as milk monitor when I led my first crusade against waste. Margaret Hilda, said a little voice inside me, have you forgotten what God put you on this earth to do? I suddenly found that I could not look that honest milk-man in the face, and then and there I resolved that I would do something about it.

As with so much of my career, the rest is history. In the House that very afternoon I announced that there would be no more free school milk. Of course there was an uproar of feigned indignation from the so-called Labour members, so much so that the second half of my sentence was drowned out, and nobody heard it. The result was that I was immediately branded as a 'milk-snatcher' in the gutter press. Of course, nobody wanted to hear what I had really said: that I had no objection at all to children *buying* milk if they were so minded, just as I had had to do as a girl. Indeed, I was all for it; it would be an incentive for them to get little jobs delivering newspapers or sweeping chimneys, and that way they would get into the habit of working at a much earlier age.

I smile now when I read the latest scientific reports, which prove conclusively how bad milk is for you, being so full of cholesterol. If only I had known that at the time! But it has often been the case in my political life that I have said something and only found out that it was true later; it's a sort of sixth sense I have, and it has served me faithfully throughout my career (in the *Belgrano* incident, to name but one instance). I explain it this way: I believe

that I instinctively know what is right for other people –
perhaps it's all part and parcel of being a mother – and so I
know what people really need and want quite some time
before they do themselves. This remarkable talent is a
godsend because I can reassure myself that whatever I
decide to do must be not merely right but my duty.

Once I found out the truth about how bad milk is for
you, incidentally – and this will, I hope, show you
exactly what sort of woman I am – I found that I couldn't
rest easily at night for worrying about it. I felt that, in
spite of all my achievements, there was more I could do
to take care of my neighbour. As it happened at the time,
my immediate neighbour was Geoffrey Howe, and the
thought of poor Geoffrey, with his weight problem,
being subjected to the temptations of gold-top first thing
in the morning was more than I could bear. So nothing
would do but I had to get up, put on my slippers and
dressing-gown, creep out at half past five and remove
the milk bottles from his doorstep. Poor man, I don't
suppose he even noticed!

'Look after the pennies,' Father used to say, 'and the
pounds will look after themselves.' But while I was
saving the pennies at Education, Ted was squandering
the pounds in a most deplorable way. To give you one of
many, many examples, he insisted on dragging us into
the Common Market. As a shopkeeper's daughter, I
have always had a healthy mistrust of markets of all
kinds, which do nothing but harm to ordinary retailers. I
clearly remember how angry Father used to get when he
saw the prices that the gypsies charged for their fruit and
vegetables in Grantham market. 'Just look at that,' he
would say. 'If things go on like this, I'll have to take a
farthing a hundredweight off spuds, and that'll be you
and your mother in the workhouse!' I often think of that
when I attend summit meetings to discuss the Common
Agricultural Policy.

Worse still, Ted Heath even wanted to dig a tunnel
under the Channel, to make it easier for the French to get
at us. I shudder to think what Henry the Fifth would have
made of that! Poor Ted and his tunnel – he simply didn't
have the vision that I have. Even then, I realised that a
publicly-funded Channel Tunnel would be an absolute
disaster. The only way in which the idea could be made to
work would be for *private* money to be poured into it.
Under Heath, the whole point of the tunnel was some
nebulous idea about improving trans-European links and
uniting the Continent with Great Britain. It took me to
see that the only possible justification for such a venture
was to make a profit. You see, that way even if the whole
idea fails to get off the ground, the Government will be
able to buy the freehold at a knock-down price, and then
we'll have a ready-made one-way sewage outflow which
will take the pressure off our overstretched waterworks –
to say nothing of being able to get at least some of our
own back on the French for boycotting English lamb.

Ted's general woolly-mindedness was bound to get
him into trouble. He simply couldn't bear to leave things
alone. Just look at the things he fiddled with! For one
thing, he messed about with all the borders of the
counties, with the result that Rutlandshire – a Conservative stronghold for centuries – disappeared off the
face of the map. Then, for some reason best known to
himself, he decided to scrap the old system of pounds,
shillings and pence in favour of so-called decimal money.
Another disaster! Some people even now have difficulty
making head or tail (if you'll pardon the pun!) of the new
system; Nigel Lawson, to name but one. (Between you
and me, left to himself Nigel would be far happier if we
all used cowrie shells.) As a result of Ted's misguided
brainstorm, the dear old tanner and threepenny-bit
became things of the past, and we were lumbered with
these horrible new coins with no proper names. And

look what it's done to the standard of arithmetic in our schools. When I was a girl I could tell you in a flash how much change you would get out of half-a-crown if you bought a shilling and fivepence farthing's worth of tea. But Ted insisted that shopping would be so much easier if everything was calculated in units of ten; presumably because he had never got out of the habit of counting on his fingers. He also moves his lips when he reads, sliding his finger along the lines. He didn't go to a very good school.

Incidentally, while I'm on the subject, I must mention that people are always nagging me to have my head put on our coins instead of Her Majesty's. It's true that I have a better profile than ER (as I affectionately call her), and I have occasionally found myself doodling trial designs on the back of Cabinet minutes. But, as Denis rightly points out, one hardly likes to think of the things people do with coins – levering off jam-jar lids or drilling holes in them to make washers. How would *you* like to have your head shoved in a ticket machine at Oxford Circus tube station?

It soon became clear that Ted's grip on reality was not too good at the best of times. On many occasions he would lapse into a sort of waking dream in the middle of Prime Minister's Question Time and start humming little tunes to himself, and once during a debate on the Finance Bill he turned to Reginald Maudling and asked him if Easter was late again this year. I imagine that his being a bachelor had something to do with it and his attitude to women seems to bear this theory out. The best example of this, of course, was his attitude to me, as the only woman of calibre in the Government. Despite the excellent job I was doing at Education, he persisted in refusing to promote me, even to a relatively lowly post such as Foreign Secretary. The only possible explanation for this is that he distrusted all women on principle.

As a general rule, it must be said, I disapprove of

unmarried MPs: they lack the stability that a happy marriage should bring. Another case in point is poor Norman St John Stevas, who I was reluctantly forced to dismiss from my Cabinet for what I can only describe as sheer wilful disobedience. If only he had married that nice ladyfriend of his – I think she was called Dorothy something – he might now be enjoying a responsible junior post in the Northern Ireland Office.

Instead of doing the decent thing and finding himself a good woman, poor Ted preferred to spend his time messing about in boats. He had a framed picture of *Morning Cloud* on his desk at Number Ten, while the bathrooms at Chequers were full of little plastic yachts which could actually be made to float if you filled the washbasin right up. His obsession with boating interfered with everything he did, and in the end he insisted that we called him 'Cap'n' at Cabinet meetings instead of 'Prime Minister'.

Now I wouldn't like you to think that, in spite of all his faults, weaknesses and aberrations, I wasn't steadfastly loyal to poor Ted as long as he was leader of the Party. Needless to say, he had my staunch support at all times, even when he was at his most unbalanced. Regrettably for him, he is entirely lacking in loyalty, and ever since I became leader he has done his level best to undermine my position. Fortunately, the best man won, and I for my part am physically incapable of bearing grudges, particularly towards a rather sad (I might almost say pathetic) character like Ted Heath. Poor man! Even though he's on his last legs he's still trying to get one over me.

The early seventies were a time of great disruption, at home and abroad. There was the Yom Kipper War (an unfortunate conflict with Iceland over fishing rights, as I remember) which led to an oil embargo. This didn't affect me particularly, as I have always used lard and

dripping instead of oil, but typically enough Ted managed to convert this minor inconvenience into a major
crisis. The result was spiralling inflation, and the whole
sorry mess came to a head in the winter of 1973, when the
country was put on a three-day week. At the time I
thought this was another of Ted's idiotic changes – after
all, he had messed about with the boundaries and the
coinage; the calendar was about the only thing he hadn't
tried to modify – but Denis explained it to me and I saw at
once what a short-sighted move it was. Denis claimed
that he was all in favour of the three-day week, which he
regarded as an extended weekend. This puzzled me, since
Denis seems allergic to Monday mornings, when he
frequently suffers from migraine.

Ted's suggestions grew pottier and pottier. For instance, he said that we should all brush our teeth in the
dark to save electricity. I remember vividly trying to
explain to him that this could cause havoc, since nobody
would be able to tell if they were using their own
toothbrush or their husband's, but of course he refused to
listen. Next he started a campaign to Switch Off Something. I willingly joined in that when he made a Party
Political Broadcast! Finally, he got in such a muddle that
he forgot that he was supposed to be running the country
and started thinking that the National Union of Miners
were the Government instead of the Conservative Party.

I would like to take this as an example of the difference
between Ted Heath and myself. In 1984, a man called
Arthur Scargill – whom I wittily dubbed Scarface, like
the other famous gangster – organised a miners' strike
with the avowed intention of overthrowing the Government. Never once did I contemplate ordering people to
brush their teeth in the dark, or anything of the sort. I
knew that the miners had to be resisted. The Falklands
War taught me that when someone wants a fight, you
must be prepared to let them have a fight, and then see

how they like it! In fact, the only difference was that the miners were British (except the Welsh ones, of course) and so should have known better – and they didn't have any battleships.

Actually, I had foreseen the conflict with the miners for quite some time and for that reason I kept Peter Walker in the Cabinet, just in case. You see, as I have said so often, I prize loyalty above almost everything else, and so if I had put a man to whom I owed any loyalty whatsoever in charge of the miners' strike, I would have been in a dreadfully difficult position if it had proved necessary to sacrifice him at some stage in the campaign. Obviously I couldn't care less what happened to Peter Walker (who could?) and so my freedom of manoeuvre was completely unrestricted. When I finally won the strike, I was able to send him to the Welsh Office (where he remains to this day, for all I know) and thus preserved my Cabinet intact. As Denis said at the time, I counted them all out and I counted them all back.

The victory over the miners wasn't just a personal triumph for me; it was a triumph for democracy. What was basically at stake, you see, was my trade union reform legislation, of which I feel justifiably proud. For the first time in history, trade unions are now obliged to ballot their members and to keep on balloting them until they get the right answer and go back to work. Left to themselves, without this safeguard there's no knowing what they might vote for. But that was not the only point at issue. There was also the matter of redundant pits. What Mr Scarface failed to grasp – he wasn't a very intelligent man – was that there were simply too many miners in too many mines. It took the strike to convince the nation of this – we found, of course, that we could manage perfectly well on the coal that the non-striking pits produced, with a little help from imports from South Africa to tide us over. Finally, the strike gave millions of people throughout the country a wonderful opportunity to see our magnificent police force in action in the face of almost inhuman violence, and as a result I was able to do what I had been wanting to do for years and raise police wages by an average of 128 per cent with the help of overtime pay. In fact, my abiding memory of those stirring days in 1984 is of our gallant boys in blue, mounted on their splendid chargers, galloping to the rescue like the Fifth Cavalry. It only goes to show that every ill wind has a silver lining.

But in 1973 my crowning glory was still to come. Ted Heath's bungling mismanagement so confused the voters that in the end they were unable to tell the difference between Labour and Conservative, with the result that when a General Election was called, many people voted the wrong way by mistake and the Conservatives were left without an absolute majority. In a typically underhand and undemocratic move, the Labour Party formed a coalition with the Liberals and bribed the miners back to work.

In the face of this national disaster, I knew where my first duty lay; yet how could I square this with my duty to my leader? This was my dilemma – my duty to my leader versus my duty to the Party, the country and, above all, my destiny. It was a terrible choice to be confronted with, but as usual I was able to see quite clearly what had to be done.

CHAPTER SEVEN

Send Her Victorious

As soon as the country had recovered from the shock of finding itself, nominally at least, under the heel of a Labour Government, the Party set about the task of preparing for the next election.

It was obvious that the defeat, however theoretical, had finally snapped poor Ted Heath's already tenuous link with the real world. What better evidence of this can you ask for than the fact that, with a Shadow Cabinet to assemble, he entrusted me with nothing more significant than the Environment? For those of you who aren't politically aware, I must explain that the Environment is very big and, by and large, more trouble than it's worth. One of its main ingredients is Housing, and Ted had decided, no doubt in a desperate attempt to preserve his grip on the leadership, to handicap me with the most idiotic policies he could think of. For one thing, I was forced to promise to keep interest rates artificially low, down as far as 9½ per cent, regardless of what the market might say. I was brought up from my mother's knee to believe that interest rates are the lifeblood of the economy, and that any attempt to tamper with them is flying in the face of nature.

However, I made the best I could of the job which Ted's shortsighted thinking had landed me with. I have always been a passionate believer in home ownership, and I practise what I preach, since I have no less than three homes – four, if you include my bunker. For a start, there's Number Ten. Of course, strictly speaking this is no better than a tied cottage (so you see, I *do* understand the problems of dilapidated public housing and noisy neighbours) but I intend to change that. After all, now that every Tom, Dick or Harry has the right to buy his council house, why shouldn't Denis and I buy Number Ten? We've lived there for well over the minimum period for council dwellers under the 1985 Housing Act, and so we should be entitled to the maximum discount. In fact, Denis has already gone so far as to apply for outline planning permission to build a small office block in the garden. With his truly entrepreneurial spirit, Denis is an inspiration to me at all times.

Then there's Chequers, our little place in Buckinghamshire. That too is public property, in theory at least; but without breaking too many confidences I might as well tell you that ER has set her heart on giving it to us as a little retirement present when we finally decide to call it a day. And when you think of it, it really is the least she can do, considering the trouble that rather peculiar son of hers has caused me over the years.

Finally, there's our house in Dulwich, a magnificent real imitation Georgian mansion, of which we are both extremely fond. In fact Denis has even given it a nickname; he calls it his little Capital Gain. It's a shame that we won't be able to live there for years yet, but thanks to the 1988 Housing Act we'll be able to let it out for an extremely good rent and be sure of being able to evict the tenants like a shot just as soon as we need it for ourselves.

So, as you can see, I am firmly committed to property ownership for all sections of the community. This made it all the harder for me to try and propagate Ted's scatterbrained policies, and I spent most of the summer of 1974 pretending to believe in something that I knew was nonsense. Mark my words, it's one of the most exhausting things you can set yourself to do – no wonder Denis Healey had bags under his eyes when he was Labour's Defence spokesman!

Inevitably, the Labour Government collapsed, and another election was called. Only one thing stood between us and overwhelming victory. Unfortunately, no one had had the courage to tell Ted what it was, and so he bumbled his woolly way through the campaign, totally unaware of the harm he was doing. As that marvellous Scotch wit Oscar Wilde would have said, 'To lose one election in a year may be regarded as a misfortune; to lose two means you get the sack.' With the possible exception of Edwina Currie, the one thing the Conservative Party cannot abide is a loser, and Ted had single-handedly thrown away two God-given opportunities to sling the socialists out of power and give the people what they really wanted.

As soon as that sorry episode was behind us, we all started thinking about who was to succeed to the leadership of the Party. Apart from myself, the obvious choice at that stage was Keith Joseph, a man so like me in so many ways that at times I find it hard to tell the difference between us. He too has a remarkable intellect, although when his brain starts to work you can see the veins throbbing on his forehead like a trafficator while his eyes bulge in a most impressive manner. But although he was virtually my equal intellectually, he could never hope to match me in sensitivity and understanding. So although we had the same influences and read the same books (though he read them in the original German), he was never able to communicate his ideas in the wonderfully clear and comprehensible way that I do. Unlike me, he has never learned how to talk down to people.

In October that year he made a speech about Government expenditure at Birmingham in Lancashire. As it turned out, he had discussed the topic with me only a few days before, over a cup of Bovril in Flood Street, and it was only natural that he should subconsciously find himself making some of the points I had impressed upon him, particularly my theory about how best to discourage the working classes from excessive breeding. It has to be said that Keith very nearly ruined those ideas for all time by his cack-handed presentation of them.

The gist of my hypothesis was this. It had started as a discussion about education. We had agreed that a first-class education is the birthright of every child, but that mass schooling in comprehensive schools (or concentration schools, as I wittily dubbed them) was utterly counterproductive. Since it is a fact of life that only the better-off can afford to send their children to proper schools, the only real hope for common folk is that their children will go to good old-fashioned grammar schools. On the other hand, with the best will in the world there are only so many places at grammar schools (which is how it should be) and any fool can tell you that what the problem boils down to is too few places for too many children. Since it would be impossible to increase the number of places without lowering the standards to an unacceptable extent, the only option would be to reduce the number of children.

At the time I remember being very much taken with this idea, which someone humorously nicknamed Operation Herod; but just as we were about to continue our discussion to its logical conclusion I had to dash out and switch off the gas under the turnips and by the time I got back Keith had gone away to some meeting or other, with the idea still only half-baked in his mind.

The next I knew of it was the banner headlines in the gutter press. Of course, they distorted every word of his speech, but it appears that he said that people in the social classes C and D should be given contraceptives to stop them having children. Keith had failed to understand the key point of my argument entirely. Obviously you can't forbid common people to have children; it would be a total abnegation of human rights. All that one can do in a democracy is to punish them if they persist in doing so. That is what I would have told him if he had stayed to listen, and that of course is what I have been trying to achieve by freezing child benefit and doing away with Family Income Supplement ever since. And I would never have suggested that the Government *give* anything to anybody. If the man on the street wants contraceptives, he should buy them like everybody else!

Anyway, the press uproar meant the end of Keith's hopes of leading the Party. Of the other contenders, Edward du Cann was forbidden to stand by his wife – clearly a very sensible woman – and in any event he had problems of his own at that time, since his company was in some sort of financial mess. I remember asking Denis if he would consider giving them some advice to get them out of it, and he replied that he had already done so, quite some time before. Obviously they hadn't followed it.

The only other serious contender (perhaps 'serious' isn't the right word in this context) was Willie Whitelaw. Fortunately, his sense of loyalty prevented him from opposing Ted directly. Willie is an outstandingly loyal person – he always reminds one of a great big soppy sheepdog – and so I was spared the painful task of having to deal with him at that time. Later, of course, he was to be one of my staunchest allies, and since he was never one to cause trouble by thinking too much for himself, I found him an extremely useful member of the Cabinet. As my mother used to say of me when I was a baby, he was so little trouble you hardly knew he was there.

To return to 1974. It soon became clear that nobody was man enough to do what was necessary and get rid of Heath. With one exception. In November, I finally, rather reluctantly, allowed my name to appear on the nomination papers.

During the campaign I spent a lot of time on the Finance Bill which was then going through the Commons. My short way with the Labour Party reminded me irresistibly of the old mince-grinding machine we had in the shop in North Parade; you put bits of old stale bread and scraggy ends of meat in one end and out came lovely fresh mince at the other. While I was wreaking havoc with the Labour front bench, Ted just sat there looking like a melting snowman, unable to do anything at all. He was now so far gone that he started canvassing Labour backbenchers for their support in the leadership ballot – poor Brian Walden was most upset.

By now there were three candidates: myself, Ted and a Scotch aristocrat called Hugh Fraser who I think had entered his name in the belief that the ballot was a raffle. As his idea of canvassing consisted solely of singing 'Glasgow Belongs To Me' in the House of Commons bar, I was able to disregard him. At least his campaign message was partially true, which was a good deal more than one could say for Ted's paranoid ramblings.

I took my campaign to the press. I even gave an interview to *Pre-Retirement Choice*, a magazine for the elderly, since I could be sure that the greater part of Ted's Cabinet were regular readers of it. I remember that I said that while inflation was high, pensioners would be wise to stockpile high-protein food such as salmon, sardines and ham, just as I did. And still do, let me add; at the back of the larder at Chequers I have the tin of pre-war Spam that my mother gave me as a wedding present.

The gutter press were quick to call me a 'hoarder'. My only reply to that was that if 'hoarding' is the same thing as taking sensible precautions against such eventualities as miners' strikes, oil embargoes and nuclear war, then it's a shame that there isn't more of it about. I pointed out

I was most distressed to find chewing gum under the arm
of the Speaker's chair.

Guess who rules the waves?

One small cone for myself; one Jumbo 99 for mankind.

Ponting, Tisdale, Wright: if you want a job doing well, do it yourself.

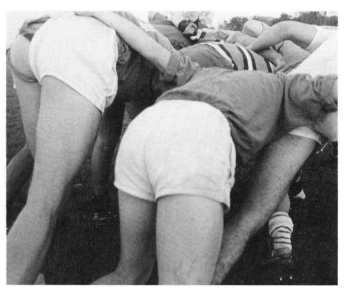

Denis (left) as I first knew him.

I was lucky to find such a steadfast constituency.

I prize loyalty above all virtues.

Myself with man and woman (unidentifiable).

Good taste is timeless.

At ease with the younger generation.

Once a grocer's daughter . . .

My hero!

Our birthright: freedom of speech.

that tins of baked beans were just as much a part of our heritage as paintings and statues (more so, actually; I don't know if you're aware of this, but the vast majority of the objects on display in the so-called British Museum are in fact imported. Scandalous! No wonder so many of them are falling to bits). Tins of rice pudding piled high in the shops of Great Britain sum up our glorious country for me as the Land of Plenty. Even this can be a mixed blessing. I remember that during the Falklands War I had to keep a top SAS team stationed in Britain just to break into supermarkets and strip the little tin keys off the sides of cans of Argentinian corned beef, to stop people buying them. Needless to say, they achieved their mission in the face of great perils and were each awarded a special medal for their contribution to the glorious victory.

Success in the first ballot did not guarantee me the leadership. Many of you will not be old enough to remember a Conservative leadership election, and if I tried to explain how the procedure worked you would think it very odd indeed (it was thought up by Alec Douglas-Home one afternoon when he was up to his waist in some Scotch trout-stream). However, my campaign manager worked out how to deal with all the quirky little procedural steps and hit on the cunning idea of spreading a rumour that I would only get seventy votes. The result was that my actual poll went up considerably, since people who felt they couldn't vote for me if there was any chance of my winning (because of some misguided loyalty to Ted) were able to vote for me with clear consciences. Predictably poor Ted came a very poor second and, for once in his life, did the right thing and resigned (although I believe he spelt his name wrong in his letter of resignation). Just then we were all able to take a welcome break from politics by spending a week at the Young Conservative Conference at Eastbourne. Since both Willie and I would inevitably be there, the photographers insisted on taking a photograph of us together, and demanded that he should give me a kiss! I was quite perplexed at this until my campaign manager pointed out that since everyone knew I never permitted anyone to kiss me on the cheeks, Willie would have no option but to bend down and kiss my ring. Of course he looked so silly that no one could take him seriously after that.

I remember very well hearing the result of that ballot. It was Airey Neave who came to break the news to me. He came into my room and said, 'Well, Margaret,' (he always called me Margaret), 'you're leader of the Opposition.' Of course I was stunned, since I thought he meant that I'd lost, but once he had explained it to me I felt jubilant. As I recall, I said 'I will be good'.

Willie was the perfect gentleman, as ever and once the leadership issue was resolved I felt it would be best to make him deputy leader until the time came when I could safely shunt him off to the Lords. As it turned out he proved to be a highly trustworthy and competent minister at the Home Office. He also made a very good cup of tea and always knew exactly where I had left things, like handbags or slippers. When the time came to have him 'put to sleep' (as the funny saying goes) I felt the least I could do was make him a viscount.

I remember well that when I was vetting his memoirs before they went to the publisher, I came across the following passage, which I am sure he would be glad to share with you here:

> Let me say just this, and I say this in all sincerity, because from the very moment when she first became leader of the Opposition of the day, and even before that, Margaret has, and I hope always will, possess the qualities and strengths, without any of the weaknesses, which, under present circumstances, together with, I may add, any unforeseen circumstances which may arise in the future,

could, should and I think I can most definitely say *would*,
all things being equal, allow her and those around her and
those who support her, as I always have, whatever slight
differences may have arisen between us in the past, and I
sincerely hope that she has forgotten all about them, as I
have, since it is absolutely essential for the well-being not
only of the Party as a whole but the country as well that
we should now be in a position to move forward without
looking back, and on to new horizons – and let us be in no
doubt that there will be new horizons to look forward to,
in the very near future if not now at this present moment,
since after all is said and done it is to the future that we
must look, which leads me inevitably to say that I believe
that Margaret has, in her own steadfast and inimitable
way, prepared not only herself but her children, and her
children's children, for those tasks which confront us now
and will confront us in days to come, and may I add that I
and all those I have come across and others too whom I
have not personally met but who have made themselves
known to me over the years from all sides of the political
spectrum, have always found her to be not only a charming, pleasant and above all a pleasure and a privilege to
work with and work for.

I don't know if this passage appeared in the published
version but I should like to think it did. Norman St John
Stevas described my success a little bit more succinctly by
saying, 'It wasn't an election, it was an Assumption.'

Far be it for me to reawaken the raw wounds of the
seventies. It is wonderful to reflect that there is now a
generation of young people growing up in Britain who
have never known and never will know what it is like to
live under a Labour Government. Winters of discontent,
the IMF running the country, mass unemployment, the
Health Service on the verge of collapse, riots in the inner
cities – all these nightmares became a thing of the past on
May 3rd 1979, when a new age dawned in Britain –
indeed, in the world at large.

Only posterity will be able to know exactly how fundamental was the revolution I achieved on that day. The election itself passed off without too many problems since the real battle had already been won when I kicked out poor old Ted. The campaign was therefore little more than a prolonged celebration of the start of the new era. I was firmly resolved to enjoy it, and enjoy it I did. I can remember having great fun at one photocall holding a newborn calf. I assumed at first that one should hold it by the ears, but the farmer suggested an equally good alternative.

By midnight it was clear that the victory was going to be of suitably impressive proportions. When the moment finally came, my mind went back to an interview I once gave to a current affairs programme called *Blue Peter*, in which I said that it would be years before a woman would either lead the Party or become Prime Minister. 'I don't see it happening in my lifetime,' I said. Everyone who knows me will bear witness to the fact that on the rare occasions when I am proved wrong I am the first to admit it, and so if I was asked the same question now, I would have to say 'I don't suppose there'll be another Prime Minister in my lifetime.'

At that moment of triumph, however, my thoughts were far away from the spotlight of history that I had just entered. Even as the first deafening whoops of jubilation arose from every side, I was reflecting that now I could never go back to that little shop in North Parade. Gone for ever were my dreams of being just another housewife and mother doing her God-given duty at the sink and the ironing-board. What, I wondered, would become of my family, without me to cook and clean for them? Who would polish Denis's golfing shoes, or darn the holes in Carol's tights? Who would Mark bring his washing home to at weekends? I shed a silent tear as I thought of all the things, a woman's birthright, that I would be forced to go without. Never again would I be able to push my trolley round the supermarket or spend a whole morning peacefully turning the collars on my husband's shirts. And yet, I reflected, I had not lost a family, I had gained one. All of Britain was my family now, and I was responsible for keeping the whole place clean and tidy and properly run, with the housekeeping money sensibly spent and a little bit put by for a rainy day or the South Atlantic. I was a mother still; I was now the Mother of the Country.

CHAPTER EIGHT

Rejoice, Rejoice

On the afternoon of 4th May 1979 I received a telephone
call from Sir Philip Moore. This was no ordinary call and
when the operator asked if I would accept the charge I
readily agreed as Sir Philip was the Queen's secretary –
typical of ER to have a man for a secretary, I always
think. I only hope he makes a reasonable cup of coffee!

I arrived at Buckingham Palace just under four minutes later. I remember looking about me when I arrived
and reflecting on just how far I had come from North
Parade, Grantham. Certainly the palace is quite unlike
the little flat over the shop where I first came into the
world – for a start, it's considerably larger. However, I
do feel that with a little imagination it could be made
quite cosy and home-like. All one would need would be
patience, a little flair, and plenty of loose covers.

I was immediately asked to form a government. I
kissed Her Majesty's ring and from that second onwards
I was Prime Minister. I shall always recall those moments
with mixed feelings. Obviously I was pleased and relieved to have fulfilled my destiny at last; but I couldn't
help noticing as I kissed the ring that ER bites her
fingernails. I made one or two suggestions that should
help her get out of the silly habit, such as smearing her
fingers with onion or garlic or rubbing them in an ashtray
every morning, and I was pleased to note that Her
Majesty was impressed by my advice. I have heard it said

that ER is not very good at taking advice, but this is not true – just so long as the suggestion is put to her in a way that she can understand!

Ever since then, I am delighted to say, we have had an excellent working relationship. As is usual in any business partnership, we have had our little differences, at least until I have had an opportunity to explain my point of view in detail. For example, I drafted an Immigration Bill that would mean that just because a man marries a British citizen he does not automatically acquire British nationality; the logical thing would have been to make this measure retrospective, postdating it to 1947. However, when I put this to ER at one of our regular chats she immediately changed the subject and began talking excitedly about knitting patterns. It was only later that Denis explained to me that the result of the proposal would be that the Duke of Edinburgh would have had to be deported to Greece. On this occasion I felt it best to give a little, since I have always been prepared to make exceptions to every rule on humanitarian grounds. Fortunately, I could never be placed in such a difficult position, having had the foresight to marry an Englishman.

Occasionally I have found that ER has tried to go one better than me. She lacks modesty. 'Prime Minister,' she will say (she always calls me Prime Minister), 'we feel rather tired today, since so far this week we have opened three hospitals.'

'Really?' I generally reply. 'What a coincidence. *We*'ve closed down four only this morning.'

But I mustn't say more about our audiences, as they are called, since that would be contrary to all the rules of protocol. Nevertheless, I must put it on record that I have found ER a great source of comfort and support at times. It is, after all, a tremendous relief to be able to talk things over occasionally with a woman who can understand my hopes and fears and who I needn't talk down to. Although we obviously cannot talk as equals – with the best will in the world, nobody could say that ER has achieved half as much as I have – I have come to value our cosy woman-to-woman chats very much. I have even passed on some of my mother's most precious recipes, although strictly speaking they should never leave the family! Still, I tend to think of ER as family, in a way. Father would have got on well with her, too; he would have admired her innate sense of frugality. To give you an example, whenever I call, she invariably orders tea for one (that's not just her funny way of speaking; I mean she orders only one cup of tea). She must have heard somewhere that I don't drink tea before four-thirty, and she clearly can no more abide waste than I!

To return, however, to that fateful day. I left Buckingham Palace for 10 Downing Street as Prime Minister of Great Britain – incidentally, I should just like to point out that the ill-informed people who say that I know nothing of the problems of inner cities couldn't be more wrong; I have now lived for ten years in the very middle of the biggest city in Britain, so I probably know a great deal more about the subject than they do – and as I drove those few hundred yards my mind was filled with doubt. What was I going to say as I made my first entrance into what had been my spiritual home for so many years? My son Mark suggested something about 'boldly going where no woman has gone before'; I considered that for a moment, but I felt it would be a dreadful omen to split an infinitive on such an auspicious day. Ronnie Millar suggested some lines from Francis of Assisi, the well-known nineteenth-century Italian playwright. I wish I could remember them – they're right on the tip of my tongue – but since the verses didn't contain any facts or statistics they have completely gone from my mind. Something about there being conflict and error, I think;

he must have meant it as a reference to the Labour Party! Then, as so often before, inspiration came to me and I walked into my new home with the words 'There is work to be done'. And indeed there was! The previous occupants, an elderly couple called Mr and Mrs Callaghan, had left the place in a terrible state. There were dog hairs everywhere, and my fingers were itching to take down the curtains and give them a good long soak.

But I decided that that would have to wait until I had formed a Cabinet. Admittedly, at the first Cabinet meeting we did spend the first half-hour polishing the table and giving the Cabinet Room a good spring-clean, but that was understandable. The place was virtually uninhabitable, what with stale sandwich crusts, half-empty glasses of beer and specks of ash from where someone had been smoking a pipe.

At that time, I must explain, I felt it necessary to keep up the pretence of Cabinet Government. Although I was not going to waste time with internal arguments, I felt that if we went through the motions of debate, even having a little 'vote' at the end, it would help my Ministers feel the degree of involvement that encourages people to take their work seriously. I believe the people who run management training courses call it a role-playing exercise, or something of the sort. So you see, when I say that I am firmly committed to shop-floor input into management decision-taking, these are not mere idle words. Besides, while they're all chattering away and having their show of hands, I can decide what I'm actually going to do.

Most of the early part of my first term was dominated by something called 'monetarism'. This concept may seem unfamiliar to you, so I had better explain that it is nothing more complicated than what you and I now call Thatcherism. I have already been through the elements of this way of solving problems — when I was talking about making ice-cream fluffier at J. Lyons – but if I may recap, the intention behind it is to create as many small businesses as possible. In the early 1980s we got off to a flying start and created a huge number of small businesses, mainly by starting off with big ones. One of my achievements that gives me particular satisfaction is the enormous number of one- or two-man concerns that have sprung into life during my time in power. All it takes, I always say, is nerve, commitment, and a little bit of redundancy money to turn a semi-efficient employee into a thriving entrepreneur, working every hour God sends, just as Father used to do.

One amusing by-product of that first period of frantic activity was my very first catch phrase. Nowadays, so many of my little sayings have become part of everyday speech that I no longer notice them, but I think the earliest was 'The lady's not for turning'. Actually, it originated in a slight slip of the tongue. It was during one of those group photographs at some summit conference in New York or Geneva or some such foreign place, and the photographer (a foreigner) can't have known my name, since he called out 'Could the lady in the front row turn a little bit to the right, I can't quite see the President because of her hat.' I meant to say 'The lady isn't turning, thank you very much' but then the Sultan of somewhere or other trod on my heel and it came out all wrong. Anyway, the rest is history.

On the global front, I was having a little trouble with Rhodesia. To be honest with you, at that stage I tended to get Rhodesia and South Africa rather muddled up; I knew that they were both civilised countries in the bottom part of Africa, near the pointed end, but beyond that I couldn't really tell them apart. Then a funny little man called Muzorewa (I can't remember his proper name, but his nickname was 'Bishop' – he wasn't a real bishop, of course; after all, he was black) suggested that I might be able to tell them apart if we called one of them something different. I remarked that it would have to be something very different indeed to do any good, and he at once suggested the name Zimbabwe. I had to admit that it was extremely different! Anyway, it worked and I've never confused the two countries since. I'm particularly happy about the way Zimbabwe has progressed politically ever since under its new leader, President Ian Botha. He seems a very sensible man with whom I can do business, and of course I vividly remember watching him playing cricket for England. It's remarkable what you can do just by changing the name of something. We stopped Windscale being dangerous just by calling it Sellafield, and we got rid of the Liberals once and for all when they were renamed the SLD.

In 1981, I must confess, a new man entered my life. His name was Ronald Wilson Reagan, and meeting him was the dream of my girlhood come true since I had fallen in love with him the first time I saw him advertising cigarettes on the back cover of some American magazine. I was his first visitor after his inauguration as President of the United States and our relationship has been very close. One year he even sent me a Valentine card which was signed with a loving kiss, and although a man from the American Embassy tried to make out that this was how he often signs his name, especially early in the morning, I knew what it really signified. From the very start we were on first-name terms; I asked him to call me Margaret and he asked me to call him Bronco. We only ever disagreed once on matters of policy, and that was over the technology for Star Wars. Although I tried my best to explain to him that the light sabres were nothing but a clever special effect, he wouldn't believe me, and he actually asked his aide Colonel North to order five thousand of them for the Marines before he found out that I had been right all along. As I said to him, 'I'm a chemist, Ronnie. I know about these things.' Even then, I think he was confused. He asked me if I could let him have something for his indigestion.

In the summer of 1981 we had some disagreeable happenings on the domestic front. A great many honest shopkeepers had their windows smashed by hooligans – though not, I am delighted to say, in Grantham. The trouble was mostly in isolated pockets – places like Brixton in Manchester, Brookside in Liverpool and Toxteth in Birmingham. Naturally I sped to the scene to offer a shoulder for the victims to cry on (I borrowed an old coat from my chauffeur's wife) and was in a position to render much practical assistance as well, since I was able to tell them exactly how to touch up their fire-damaged stock the way Father used to do, so that nobody would ever know the difference.

I recall that on the night of the disturbances in Toxteth I spent the early part of the evening at the theatre. I had been given tickets to see a play called *Anyone for Tennis?*, with a man called John Wells in it. It was a rather dreary play about an alcoholic and his dreadful wife and I can't remember too much about it – I spent most of the first half answering letters and Denis fell asleep – but I do recollect that it starred a policeman, and I made a point of going 'backstage' to congratulate the actor on his performance. I said that he must be feeling very proud to be wearing the uniform of our brave guardians of law and order, but I think he was overcome with nerves (this often happens to ordinary folk when they meet me) because he made no reply.

ER shared my concern for what was going on in the inner cities, and so we arranged for her son to get married later that year, to give the ordinary folk something to cheer them up. Finding a suitable match was not easy. My first thought was Carol, but when I considered the age difference between her and Charles I reluctantly had to veto the idea; and besides, I couldn't reconcile myself to the thought of my daughter marrying a man who talks to plants. So in the end Charles had to make do with second best, and he seems to be bearing up remarkably well. As for Carol, she remains unattached. It's a pity President Reagan hasn't got a son of the right age.

There was a mix-up with the seating at St Paul's at the Royal Wedding and I ended up with a place behind a pillar that had been intended for the French Ambassador. Luckily I had my compact mirror with me, and by positioning it on the shoulder of the man in front of me – some sort of Arab, as I recall – I was able to see the whole thing. Not that it was worth the effort, in the long run. My mother would *not* have approved of those creases!

Denis and I were undecided what to get the happy couple for a wedding present. Denis, with typical generosity, suggested offering Charles a place on the board of one of his companies, but I felt that that was going a bit too far, as, when all was said and done, we didn't know them terribly well and I do dislike people who give ostentatious presents. So in the end we settled on a set of good quality saucepans. I feel strongly that a good, sturdy set of saucepans is every bride's birthright.

The second of April 1982 was one of the darkest days of my first term of office. No doubt you will be completely familiar with the events of those stirring times from your GCSE syllabus, but I would like to give you a first-hand account, as I fear that patriotic fervour may have slightly distorted some of the facts of the Falklands victory.

The Argentine dictator General Galtieri had been experiencing considerable difficulties in domestic politics, what with high unemployment, an economic crisis and riots in the streets of most of the major cities, and in a typically devious way he attempted to take the minds of the people off the realities of the situation by waging a war in a small, unimportant group of islands many,

many miles from home. He overlooked one thing in his calculations, however: the fact that the islands are British – every bit as British as Finchley or Grantham, and considerably more so than many parts of Wales I have been to on State visits.

With the help of a neat black dress and a task force I was soon able to overcome the enemy on two fronts, and once I had dealt with the Foreign Office and the Labour Party, I brought all my powers of leadership to bear on the crusade to liberate the islands. In Tennyson's words, 'I stood tall and did it my way'.

Of course, I strained every sinew to bring the conflict to an end without a shot being fired. I wrote a very strong letter to General Galtieri, which I sent by recorded delivery to make sure it reached him, and I would have given the most serious possible consideration to the Peruvian peace plan if only I hadn't left it on the seat of my official car just before it went through the carwash. Unfortunately, some fool left one of the windows open, and by the time it came out at the other end the documents were so sopping wet I couldn't read them. But I refused to be defeated by this depressing setback and wrote to Señor de Cuéllar for another copy. To give credit where it is due, he provided one, but this time I made the mistake of lending it to Sir Geoffrey Howe when he asked to borrow it (I gather he thought there was a crossword in it somewhere) and he left it at his aunt's cottage in Sittingbourne, and she mixed it up with her copies of *The People's Friend* which she sent on to her sister in New Zealand. By the time that MI6 had managed to get them back, the *General Belgrano* had made its unprovoked attack on one of our nuclear submarines, and the die was cast.

I won't give you a blow-by-blow account of the events which led up to our total victory in the Falklands crusade – my younger readers will have learned it all at their mother's knee, while anyone old enough to remember the war itself certainly won't need reminding. Suffice to say that we drove the barbaric Argies back into the sea, killing literally thousands of them with a loss to ourselves of a mere handful of Welshmen and Gurkhas and the odd ship or two. There was a small amount of Labour-inspired press hysteria about the sinking of the *Sheffield* and *Sir Galahad*; but, as I pointed out at the time, our casualties were minuscule compared to British losses in either world war (it is a matter of cold statistics that the Falklands was the most cost-effective major war in terms of British deaths per square metre recaptured since Agincourt), and since the Labour Party would doubtless have scrapped both ships long before if they had been in power, under the guise of defence cuts, they should have been only too glad to see them going down!

The other major event of 1982 was my visit to the Fitzroy Nuffield Hospital to have my varicose veins stripped. For several days the nation held its breath – I believe vigils of prayer were held in several of our cathedrals – until it was announced that the operation had been a complete success. I remember that the press saw fit to comment on the fact that I left the hospital wearing trousers. I ask you! First, I don't suppose half of these so-called journalists wear a skirt from one year's end to the next. Second, why shouldn't I wear trousers if I wish to? Metaphorically speaking, I've been wearing them for years.

It was a matter of sincere pride to me that I was able to give a helping hand to the NHS by going to a private hospital, thus enabling some poor old lady somewhere to have what would have been my bed for a long-needed hip replacement operation. So you can see that those people who claim I don't do anything about long waiting-lists are wrong, as usual. Of course, I avoid hospitals like the plague if I can, since it does no good at all if you are seen to be ill. It's a pity the Russian leaders of the time didn't follow my lead in this, or they might still be alive today.

Admittedly, in 1985 I was admitted to hospital overnight. To avoid panic and worldwide crashes on the stock exchange, the Press Office at Number Ten announced that I had a slight contracture of the hand. In fact, the simple truth was that I had under-estimated Norman Tebbit's abilities as an arm-wrestler. Apart from that, I've been content to leave the Health Service in the safe hands of a succession of capable Ministers, the best of whom has been Kenneth Clarke. He actually uses the NHS, and since he's the most overweight and unhealthy-looking member of the Government by far, it seems to me that any organisation that can keep him alive must be doing something right. The great thing about Kenneth is that he knows how to do what he's told. I only wish he wouldn't bite the newspapers when he brings them in in the mornings.

A funny little man with white hair was the leader of the Opposition at the time. He reminded me a lot of a television character from Mark and Carol's childhood called Doctor Who, and he might as well have come from a different planet for all he knew about Britain in the nineteen-eighties. His name was Michael Foot (honestly) and generally speaking, he was a nice, polite, clean old gentleman, so I didn't really approve when several of the more high-spirited Conservative backbenchers started jumping out at him in the corridors of the House and bursting paper bags, or knocking away his walking-stick (although it was all harmless fun, and he never actually seemed to notice). However, when one of them balanced a bag of wet flour on top of his office door, with the result that Mr Foot came into the Chamber for Prime Minister's Question Time covered in flour from head to foot (he hadn't noticed again, you see) I decided that these pranks had to stop, and so I called the ringleaders to my study for a gentle word of warning.

'I know what's been going on,' I said, 'and I know you're only doing your best to roll back the frontiers of socialism, but this time I think you've gone a bit far. We'll say no more about it for now, but if it happens again, I warn you that the culprit will immediately be given a junior post in the Scottish Office. And you needn't think you can get away with it by not owning up, because if you try that I'll keep the whole Party in over Henley Week. And you won't like that one little bit!'

After that, of course, the pranks stopped. But poor Mr Foot managed to make himself ridiculous without any help from the Party. I remember how embarrassed I was when he turned up at the Remembrance Day service in a donkey jacket and a pair of old overalls! Obviously he had been pottering about on his allotment, completely oblivious of the fact that he was due at the Cenotaph, and when he remembered what day it was he didn't have time to change. He looked just like one of those little men who put out the cones on the motorways, and the press were extremely rude about it all. Personally, I blame his wife for letting him go around like that.

Even in the Chamber of the House he wasn't much better. His ramblings were always a great source of amusement on the Conservative benches. Here is a representative quote from *Hansard*:

> *The Rt Hon. Michael Foot, Leader of the Opposition:* Would the Prime – ah – *Minister* in the . . . course of . . . er . . . today, or if not today, then . . . indeed, *tomorrow*, give thought and indeed due *consideration* to the . . . to the . . . give due thought and indeed *consideration* to the . . . that she, above all . . . above . . . above *all others* has and will . . . will . . . in the words of the great Nye Bevan, who said . . . who said something or other about . . . once . . . it's on the tip of my tongue, you know . . . to the effect

that . . . who *said* that those people who are *entrusted with power* and . . . er . . . responsibility – and power – should . . . er . . . endeavour [*shouts of 'Get on with it!', 'Who rattled his cage, then?', 'Hear Hear', etc*] No . . . no . . . no . . . no doubt he'd have said the same to you if you'd been born then . . . or not, as the case may be, but . . . but I will return to the question for the Right Honourable Lady . . . Lady . . . a question for the Right Honourable Lady . . . Oh let me not be mad, not mad, sweet Heaven . . . and that is . . . is . . . [*shouts of 'Give way', 'Bring out your dead', 'Hear Hear', etc*] Yes . . . Yes . . . does she agree that this and . . . er . . . er . . . *that* . . . that this and that is or are the case? Does she?

The Rt Hon. Margaret Thatcher, the Prime Minister: No

I also remember that he had a dog which always trotted obediently behind him on a lead (or perhaps it was the other way round). I can understand this, but personally I have never felt the need of a dog since I married Denis. To return to Michael Foot, however; he was such an abysmal failure that one almost felt sorry for him – until one remembered that he was a socialist, of course. I make it a point never to feel sorry for socialists since one usually finds that they are entirely to blame for their own misfortunes. I mean, there is absolutely no excuse for living in Liverpool, given that we have a perfectly adequate railway network.

The election in 1983 was more or less decided before I even announced the date. It's true that I could quite justifiably have gone to the country as soon as the Falklands crusade was finished; but I resisted the temptation, mainly for Mr Foot's sake (or rather, for Mrs Foot's sake). I realised that his Party's forthcoming defeat would mean the end of his political career, and then the poor old chap would have nothing to do all day except hang around the house getting under his wife's feet.

When I decided to write this book, I took the trouble to

look back through a few of my old scrapbooks, and I was surprised to find a great many references in the speeches and newspaper cuttings of the period to a gentleman by the name of David Owen. I must confess that although as a rule I have an almost superhuman memory for names, I have completely forgotten who this man was. From what I can piece together from my archives he was something to do with a fringe group called the Socialist Republican Movement or something of the sort, but why he was so important at the time I have no idea. If any of you readers have long memories, perhaps you could write to me at Number Ten. I have a passion for detail.

Once the 1983 election was safely out of the way and my majority had been further increased, I decided it was high time that something was done about the unions. Once I had set my hand to the plough I did not look back. However, I kept reminding myself that Britain is a free society, where people are at liberty to do anything they like, however misguided, so long as they do not infringe the law, and so I only banned them altogether in such obvious places as the Government Communications Headquarters (GCHQ).

For those of you who don't know, this is a top-secret installation in Cheltenham, just outside the town as you come from the direction of Gloucester (turn left by the Whitbread brewery and keep straight on and you can't miss it) where all the Government's intelligence comes from. Most Governments need all the intelligence they can get, and mine is no exception. Curiously enough, all this intelligence is entrusted to a lot of rather bolshy civil servants, whose job it is to translate it into language that Ministers can understand. In theory, it was under the control of Sir Geoffrey Howe, the then Foreign Secretary, and he simply had no idea how to go about stamping out the unions there. So of course I had to do it.

There was the most dreadful fuss, needless to say. The gutter press started whining about civil liberties, which was of course absurd. After all, I had just let the people have an election; what more did they want? To listen to some of these silly journalists, you'd think the people were running the country! But I took no notice, just as I always do, and soon hit upon a quite brilliantly fair and reasonable compromise.

The logic behind the proposal to outlaw unions at GCHQ was that anyone who belongs to a union is by definition a socialist, and that socialists, as is well-known, sell secrets to the Russians. I therefore offered each and every GCHQ employee £1000 as compensation for loss of potential earnings. To calculate the correct figure, I consulted the head of MI5, who told me that the going rate for British secrets in the Kremlin was £9.55 per secret, plus 45p postage & packing. In order to earn £1000 each, every GCHQ employee would have had to sell at least a hundred secrets, and these days there aren't more than fifty secrets in Britain at any one time. In fact, the market is hopelessly flooded, and it's getting to the stage where, sooner or later, the Russians won't give us a penny for anything except a good tip for the Grand National. Since I intend one day to privatise the intelligence agencies, it stands to reason that the last thing I want to do is run them down until their stock-in-trade is worthless.

GCHQ wasn't the only security problem I encountered. There was an awful fuss when the Keeper of the Queen's Pictures turned out to be a spy. Incidentally, I still don't know why ER needs a full-time member of staff just to keep her holiday snaps in order; I put all mine in a shoebox, and never have any trouble with them. Anyway, the Blunt affair had its useful side, as it kept the press happy and let me get on with running the country in the meantime.

After the Blunt affair, we had the Spycatcher non-sense. You've probably forgotten all about it by now, so I must remind you that in 1988 a rather pathetic old man, who I thought had been sent to prison but who had in fact retired to Australia (which amounts to the same thing) decided to write his memoirs. They were so bad, however, that he was unable to find a publisher in this country and so was forced to have them printed in Australia. It then turned out that this silly little man had been something to do with intelligence and had filled his book with all sorts of ludicrous allegations about MI5 interfering with members of a previous Labour Government.

The first thing I did, as you can imagine, was race round to MI5 and look through the files on the people in question. Of course there wasn't a shred of truth in any of it, although I did find out some extremely interesting (not to say entertaining) things about certain people, which I will share with you one day when I have time. Once I had satisfied myself that the allegations were false, I decided that it would be necessary to take a firm stand. I am fundamentally opposed to this deplorable tendency for public figures to write sordid and fantastic so-called autobiographies, purely and simply to make money. If I had my way, I'd have the lot of them locked up in the Tower!

Most of Peter Wright's book was taken up with him moaning about his pension. All I can say to that is that he should have paid his National Insurance contributions like everybody else. He even had the sheer effrontery to suggest that the head of MI5 had been a top KGB agent. I suppose that what I should have done was ignore the whole thing, rather than give Wright the oxygen of publicity. After all, the idea that any British civil servant could have risen to prominence in the KGB was patently absurd. I mean to say, if they were even halfway competent at anything at all, they wouldn't be in the Civil

Service to begin with, and I happen to know for a fact that the KGB are very fussy about who they pick. But as I have said, I felt that an example had to be made of Wright, and so I resolved to deal with him. Because there weren't any copies of his book in Britain, it was impossible to have them burned at Tyburn (which is what we did in Good Queen Bess's day) so the only thing left was to send Sir Robert Armstrong out to Australia to tell them not to publish it. Sir Robert is one of the few 'good' civil servants — for a start, he's economical with absolutely everything — but I don't think the natives out there could understand his English accent, because he had the most dreadful trouble making himself understood.

While I'm on the subject of MI5, I have to say that I've become rather disillusioned with them lately. Not only do they seem quite incapable of proving that Moscow funds the TUC; they tend to let their imagination run away with them when it comes to who they suspect of working for the Reds. Here, for example, is a recent list of suspects:

Enoch Powell
Bernard Levin
Rupert Murdoch
Brian Clough
Frank Muir and Denis Norden
Mavis Nicholson
Jean Alexander
Brian Redhead
William Deedes
Steve Nallon
Princess Michael of Kent
Lord Denning
Mike Gatting
Nigel Lawson
Oscar Peterson

Rod Hull & Emu
Alistair Sim
Michael Fish
Bobby Robson
Thomas à Becket
Blake Carrington
Denis Healey
Russell Grant
Dick Francis
Guy Burgess
Yves Saint-Laurent

Naturally, I checked this list with the head of the KGB, who assured me that at least three of these people had never sold him a secret in their lives. Sometimes I think they live in a world of their own.

The head of the KGB is, of course, Mikhail Gorbachev (or Mike, as I prefer to call him). I first met Mike in December 1984 when he headed the first senior Russian delegation to visit our shores for many decades. We got on like a house on fire. We had so much in common – union troubles, security leaks, irritating churchmen dabbling in politics – that we were able to talk quite freely, and I soon realised that here was a man I could do business with. I think Denis realised this too, since when I next visited Chequers I found the garage jammed with cardboard boxes full of Russian cameras and transistor radios. For my part, I tried to sell him British Leyland, but he wasn't interested. I think it was the company's dreadful history of industrial unrest that put him off, coupled with the fact that a cousin of his had once had a Metro which kept stalling at traffic lights and making a terrible whining noise in third gear. He called it his Moaning Mini.

When I heard that Mike had been made President of Russia I naturally assumed that he had only a few months to live, and so I sent him a get-well-soon card. This must have done the trick, since he seems to be as healthy as can be expected for a socialist, except for that peculiar rash on the top of his head. Once I noticed that, I found that I couldn't resist staring at it, and as a result my concentration tends to wander when we have summit conferences. I suspect that he may be allergic to fur hats. His wife is a charming woman called Raisa. Unusually for a Russian leader's wife, she weighs less than her husband, and she has at least a rudimentary dress sense.

Although Mike is obviously not as substantial a figure in world politics as I am, I have always been at pains not to stress this point when we meet, and as a result we enjoy a considerable degree of mutual respect. After all, we are striving to achieve similar objectives. Mike is doing his best to drag Russia out of the nineteenth century into the twentieth, while I am doing exactly the opposite for Britain. I have often impressed upon Mike that Britain is a proud nation. 'Mike,' I say to him, 'we British are a proud people.'

'Margaret,' he replies (he always calls me Margaret), 'that is understandable. You British achieve so much. Look how many bronze medals you win at the Olympics.'

So you can see that Mike is basically a decent person. It is a tragedy that an accident of birth made him into a socialist whose sworn objective is to undermine the freedom of the West. Had he been born into a different society – Grantham, for example – he could have made something of himself. I believe he would have had all the ingredients of a successful retailer, if he had only had the chance to prove himself.

While I am on the subject of socialism and subversion, I must just say something about the Church of England. Just as Britain was beginning to turn the tide towards the end of the tunnel, the so-called General Synod issued a pernicious little pamphlet called *Faith in the City*. When I received my copy I naturally assumed that it was a guidebook to London churches and put it in the loo at Number Ten for foreign ambassadors to read. However, it turned out to be no such thing. Masquerading under that deceptive title was a shamelessly disloyal attack on my Government's policy on the renewal of the inner cities.

As everyone knows, my formula for revitalising decaying urban areas has been a quite outstanding success. To take only one example, look at London's docklands. Not so many years ago, these were semi-derelict slums, breeding-grounds for disease and stricken with poverty. Now, however, thanks to my Government's policies, Docklands is a prosperous place where one can leave one's second car outside in the street all night without the fear of its aerial being broken off by hooligans. As soon as the right sort of people started moving there, I had no hesitation in building a railway and even an airport; so let nobody say that I have neglected the infrastructure of our cities. As I have repeatedly said, what we have done in Docklands we can do all over Britain, so long as we have the co-operation of the property developers, the estate agents, the merchant banks and the other pillars of British society.

However, the 'turbulent priests', as I jokingly call them, took it upon themselves to criticise this work of reform. Nor was it only the churchmen who did so; a prominent Atheist called David Jenkins appeared a lot on the television and presumed to talk about 'this Government's failure'. I took this to be a reference to John Selwyn Gummer, but apparently some people thought it was a comment on my social and economic policies, and I found this quite extraordinary.

As Defender of the Faith, I have the ultimate responsibility of choosing bishops. Unfortunately, the ideal

candidates such as Richard Branson and Ian Macgregor
have not been able to accept the posts I have offered them
because of other commitments. Also, like civil servants,
the senior clergy are annoyingly hard to get rid of once
they are in place – gone are the days when a dissenting
bishop could be burned at the stake! In fact, they remind
me rather of salmonella; once the little bugs are in your
tummy, the only thing you can do is starve them out, and
this is what I have been forced to resort to.

However, I delight in a challenge, and I think I have
found a way to deal with the problem. The Church of
England is, after all, nothing more than a nationalised
industry, and once one has grasped that essential fact, the
solution becomes obvious. I have already commissioned
a leading merchant bank to prepare a prospectus for
British Faith plc. The privatisation will be carried out in
the tried and tested way which has succeeded so well in
the past. To start with, all the existing employees of
British Faith plc will be offered a chance to buy shares on
favourable terms. Foreign buyers (I expect quite a strong
interest from the Italian multinationals, who have made
several unsuccessful takeover bids in the past) will have
to wait their turn until British buyers have had a chance to
sell their shares, and there will of course be a special
discount scheme for Methodists. Once the redundant
buildings have been sold off and the Pay-As-You-Pray
system is in operation, I expect British Faith plc will be
able to return a healthy profit (or should I say 'prophet'!).
Then the board will be able to do away with a number of
present unhealthy restrictive practices (the eye-of-a-
needle test, for example) and we will have a Church we
can all be proud of. I look upon the Church as another
form of Health Service, after all, and I firmly believe that
if people are prepared to work that bit harder to be able to
afford it, they have a God-given right to the best standard
of Salvation. If you want the Kingdom of Heaven,

in other words, you should be prepared to pay for it.

Now that I have touched on the subject, I would like to say that when it comes to privatisation we have only sold off the tip of the iceberg. I look forward to the day when the railways, the armed forces, the House of Lords and Scotland have all been restored to the private sector. We have already started the process with the police force, and I am presently negotiating a management buyout with James Anderton in Manchester.

I suppose you think that Westland is a fictional county in a Jeffrey Archer novel. For me it was one of my finest hours. Like Julius Caesar, I have never trusted men with long hair, and for years I had the problem of finding something for Michael Heseltine to do where he couldn't cause too much damage. I have nothing against Michael as a person (although his eyes are much too close together) but when I found out that he wanted to live in my house, I realised that he had to go. While I was trying to find some painless way of disposing of him, now that the Falklands War was over, I realised that he wasn't the only one I could well do without. Even now, when I read articles in women's magazines about getting rid of unsightly fat, I always think of Leon Brittan, and although his personal appearance was scarcely his fault, his dangerously liberal views could not be so lightly pardoned.

For reasons of national security I am not at liberty to disclose the details of the Westland Affair. This is a pity, since the letters that were never sent by me and everyone else would make a fascinating book all by themselves. However, the proof of the pudding is in the eating; and all I can say is that any Prime Minister who is given the chance to get rid of two long-standing nuisances at no more cost to the nation than the loss of a few jobs in a godforsaken place like Yeovil (which is a Liberal stronghold and thus deserves everything it gets) would be mad not to grab the opportunity with both hands. As for the argument that Britain needs helicopters for its defence, that simply doesn't hold water. Wellington didn't have any helicopters at Waterloo.

Ireland has been the bane of successive British governments for centuries, and I sometimes feel that there is no easy solution. I have done my best to find one. I recently commissioned a panel of eminent geologists to observe Ireland closely to see if it was moving. The moment it starts steering in our direction, we will have a perfect excuse to sink it in the usual way. Until then, I suppose, we will have to make do with the Anglo-Irish Pact.

I have often been told that the Irish problem stems from a lack of understanding. I cannot accept this. It's true that if all Irishmen are like John Cole, it's a miracle that anyone can understand more than one word out of every ten they say, but I fail to see how the Irish can fail to understand me. After all, I took the trouble to teach myself to speak *properly*.

Until a solution is found, however, Northern Ireland has a useful part to play in the life of Britain. Where would Cabinet reshuffles be without the threat of the Northern Ireland Office? Where else could the SAS get the experience they need with live ammunition? Without the Northern Irish problem, we might have to repeal the Prevention of Terrorism Act, which would deprive the statute book of a vital weapon against the likes of Arthur Scargill. Furthermore, we must remember that the people of Northern Ireland (or at least the Protestants) are British. Londonderry and Belfast are just as much a part of the British Empire as Port Stanley and Goose Green. Which leads me to what I consider to be the only possible solution – an invasion from the Irish Republic. Until then, we shall have to wait and see.

Another solution, of course, is to enlist the help of our

American friends. Just as we were able to help them deal with Libya, they could help us with Ulster by letting us use their airbases. The Libyan crusade, although not comparable with my achievement in the South Atlantic, was a wonderful example of what can be done by two nations who share the same dream of world peace. Article 51 of the United Nations Charter expressly authorises military action for self-defence, and I know in my heart that we acted just in time. Had we delayed a moment longer, there would have been Libyan paratroopers in the streets of Detroit. Once again, the wisdom of encouraging the Americans to station troops in this country was conclusively proved. After all, what greater reassurance could the people of Britain want than the presence of our closest allies? Heaven forbid that such a thing should happen, but in the event of a general strike, with rioting in the streets and the possibility of mutiny in the armed forces, we would be able to call on Uncle Sam to restore order and democracy, just as he did in Grenada.

During the Libyan campaign I was privileged to be able to compare my style of leadership with that other great statesman and leader of men, Ronald Reagan. Ronnie's part in the exercise was by no means that of an armchair general. In fact, he would dearly have liked to have led his brave men from the front, but unfortunately there was no time to have his horse transported to Tripoli. However, his tactical insights were as shrewd as ever, and his advice to the fighter pilots – if attacked, form the F-111s into a circle – shows what a great general he would have made had the opportunity presented itself.

In 1987 I led the Party to another effortless victory over a certain Glenys Kinnock. In a desperate attempt to win votes, the socialists had hired an advertising agency to try and brighten up their image. This cheap trick failed, needless to say; as my good friends the Saatchi brothers never tire of telling me, all the advertising in the world can't help you to sell a worthless product, unless of course you're a bank or a building society. Following their devastating rebuff in the polls, the Labour Party have now ceased to exist, and Britain is without an Opposition for the first time since the days of Charles I. In a way I rather miss the Labour Party; although they could be a nuisance at times, they tended to add a little spice of excitement to politics and I can honestly say that if it hadn't been for them, it would have been even more difficult to get rid of Ted Heath. In theory, an effective Opposition is essential for the smooth running of democracy, in that it enables the people to realise just how good the Conservatives are when they return to power. The Party, after all, is like a field; it needs to lie fallow once in a while to regain its strength and root out the weeds and the dead wood. Again, if there weren't occasional lapses of non-Conservative rule, there would be no economic crises to be solved or unions to be crushed, and people would start to become complacent.

During the election, my normally resilient constitution gave way and I was struck down with toothache. Toothache, I often feel, is like the unemployment figures; it's trivial enough in itself, but it nags away until you begin to lose all sense of proportion and start thinking that almost anything would be worth it to get rid of the pain. I held out for as long as I could, relying on my innate staunchness and some of my mother's old remedies, such as oil of cloves and newt's blood – it was difficult finding newts in central London, but someone came across a small colony of them in a cistern in the old GLC building; I can't think how they got there – but eventually I was forced to go and see a dentist. Even then, I scorned an anaesthetic as the dentist drilled away. He broke three drills before he managed to get through *my* teeth!

★

And now I am nearing the end of this part of my story. I am not a person who dwells in the past; I prefer to think of the future. Let me give you one brief example: soon we will be able to do away with rates. This is virtually a sacred cause to me. One of the last things Father said before he passed away was that the rates were a scandal and that they were driving small businesses to the wall. I have thought long and hard about how to tackle this problem, and the final solution – the Community Charge – is now nearly ready to be put into effect, following extensive testing under laboratory conditions in Scotland.

The principle behind the Charge is quite simple. It is a return not just to Victorian values but to earlier, better values still. Until the so-called reforms of the eighteenth century, the right to vote was linked directly to the individual's ability to pay. Only if a person had property – and thus a stake in the community – was he entitled to vote. This is what I am seeking to restore. Under the Charge, only people who can afford to pay will be able to register to vote. It is a lie to say that this will in any way affect the democratic system. Now that the Labour Party has gone, the poor people won't have anybody to vote for anyway.

POSTSCRIPT

We are a Grandmother

To have been in power for ten years is nothing much in itself. To have transformed one's country from little better than a third-world banana republic into the most dynamic, powerful and progressive nation the world has ever seen is admittedly a staggering achievement, but it is just conceivable that someone else in my position – Churchill, say, or Ronald Reagan – might have accomplished it. To have done all this, and never to have worn the same blouse two days in a row; that is perhaps how I would best like to be remembered.

I hope that this exceptional journey through my life history will help you to come to terms with what must at first sight seem an incredible achievement. It should also explain just why it is inevitable that I shall remain Prime Minister for the foreseeable future.

Stability, after all, is the bedrock of good government. Take the Italians, for instance. They have had nearly fifty governments since the war, and each successive regime has managed to do nothing except repeal the work of its immediate predecessor. Anyone who thinks that that is what democracy is all about is sadly wrong. Democracy should mean choosing a leader and sticking to her, through thick and thin, till death do you part. It means loyalty. It means the electorate having the common sense to trust the leader even when they don't understand what she's doing; best of all, letting her get on with the job in hand without incessant interference from the gutter press, the unions and all the other undemocratic forces at work in Britain today.

Oh, if only I could be mass-produced and exported, I'm sure we'd have the balance of trade sorted out in no time at all! I have always felt that stamina is one of the principal virtues, and of course I have more stamina than the whole of the Labour Party put together. This is in spite of being a woman. The only other female of global importance who appears to have had this essential quality is my friend the late Mrs Gandhi – although, if I may venture to criticise that excellent leader, I have always regarded being assassinated as a sign of weakness. Also, I do wish she had tried the ointment I gave her for that obstinate spot on her forehead.

What impressed me most about Indira (I always called her Indira) was her success in founding a dynasty. Of course, my own children have both chosen careers which have nothing to do with politics – Mark as a successful entrepreneur and Carol as a journalist with the *Daily Telegraph* – and in a way I am pleased that they have not tried to follow in my footsteps (particularly Mark, whose sense of direction has never been particularly strong). However, we are now a grandmother, and already I see in little Michael the potential heir to my achievement. The way in which he staunchly refuses his bottle when he has wind is a simple example. As he sits in his carrycot with his head proudly turned, he seems to be saying, 'I do not wish to drink my milk. This is a free society, and I have the right to choose. Freedom to refuse handouts which one has done nothing to earn is the hallmark of a civilised society.' Can it be an omen that he too, just like his grandmother before him, is making a stand against the very concept of free milk?

William Pitt the Elder is one of the few previous Prime Ministers of Great Britain that I have any time for. After all, he took the trouble to groom his son, William Pitt the Younger, with the result that he was Prime Minister at the age of twenty-two. Given that my own grandson is likely to be more precocious still, I can look forward to handing over the reins of power in, say, 2009 with a clear conscience. In the intervening two decades, of course, I shall have completed the various tasks that still confront me – the abolition of trade unions, the conquest of Argentina, the privatisation of Mars, the return to Victorian standards of morality and behaviour – but I feel sure that there will be plenty more for M. Thatcher the Younger to do. Perhaps, in his time, Britain will see a return to Plantagenet values with the complete restoration of the feudal system, and the Union Jack once more fluttering proudly over the palace of Versailles.

As Mr Al Jolson, the celebrated black-face entertainer, once said: 'You ain't seen nothing yet!'

Acknowledgements

Thanks are due to: Church Farm, Coombes; Granada Studio Tours; Jim Diamond (backbencher) and Ian Townsend (policeman); Royston Primary School; Peter Stringfellow; William Batstone; Tom Weldon; and Susanna Wadeson.

Photographs by Dominic Turner, with the exception of those taken at Granada Studio Tours by John Peters: *Section 1*, pages 1 above, 4 above; *Section 2*, pages 1 above, 2 below, 5, 6.

Index

advertising, 167
Alexander, Jean, 159
Americans: actresses, 6;
    airmen, 40; mutual help, 166
Anderton, James, 164
Anglo-Irish Pact, 165
Anyone for Tennis, 149
Archer, Jeffrey, 25
Argos catalogue: like Labour
    Party manifesto, 5
Armstrong, Sir Robert, 159
ARP, 41

Balliol College, 47
Barber, Anthony, 119–21
BBC: father's views of, 21;
    left-wing bias, 2, 79; radio,
    2, 21
Benn, Anthony Wedgwood,
    50–1
Bevan, Aneurin, 93
Bicester, 40
birthrate: discouraging, 134
Blue Peter, 140
Blunt, Sir Anthony, 157
Botha, Ian, 148
Boyle, Sir Edward, 117
Branson, Richard, 163
British Faith plc, 163
British Leyland, 160
British Xylonite, 54, 60–1
Brittan, Leon, 4, 28, 164
Brixton, 149
Brize Norton, 40

Broadhick, Miss, 14–15, 16,
    17–18
Brookside, 149
Buckingham Palace: potential
    as home, 143
Burgess, Guy, 160
Bush, Barbara, 113

Cabinet: definition, 103;
    dismissing members, 103;
    Government by, 108, 146;
    managing, 103, 108;
    meetings, 4; uniform for, 113
Cabinet Pudding, 113
Callaghan, James, 92–3, 146
Callaghan, Mrs, 146
canvassing, 62–5
Carrington, Blake, 160
Casson, Lewis, 86–7
catch phrases, 147
Chamberlain, Neville, 30
Changing of the Guard, 4
Channel Tunnel, 71, 124
Charles, Prince: marriage,
    149–50
Chequers, 132
children: suitable jobs for, 122
Christmas, 43–5
Christmas shopping, 4
Church of England, 161–3
Churchill, Sir Winston, 44, 52,
    64, 169
civil servants: advice from, 102;
    how to treat, 118;

civil servants – *cont.*
impossibility of being KGB
agents, 158–9
Claridge's, 100
Clarke, Kenneth, 153
clothes: buying, 112
Clough, Brian, 159
coins: having profile on, 125
Colchester, 55
Cole, John, 165
Common Market, *see* EEC
Community Charge, 168
comprehensive schools,
118–19
conscientious objectors, 38
Conservative Association:
Colchester, 57; Oxford
University, 49–52, 53–4
Conservative Party:
Conference, 59;
contributions to, 60;
leadership, 133–8
contraceptives, 134–5
cooking hints, 113–14
council meetings:
strike-breakers refused
entry, 96–7
county boundary changes, 124
Crawford, Joan, 80
Currie, Edwina, 133

Dad's Army, 41
Daily Mirror, 64; responsible for
rheumatism, 65
Daily Telegraph, 2, 57, 84, 97,
170
Dartford, 59–60, 62–5
de Cuéllar, Señor, 151
decimal currency, 15, 124–5
Deedes, William F., 97, 159
democracy, 169–70
Denning, Lord, 159
Docklands, 162
Dodds, Norman, 63
Douglas-Home, Alec (Lord
Home of the Hirsel), 109,
137

Downing Street (No. 10):
differences between
Grantham and, 12;
possibility of buying, 132;
redecorating, 3
Du Cann, Edward, 135
Dulwich, 132

Eastbourne: YC Conference,
137–8
economic theory, 99–100
The Economist, 25
economy: compared to
ice-cream, 62
Edinburgh, Duke of, 144
education: changes in, 118–20
EEC: conference, 26; joining,
123
Elizabeth, Queen: accepting
advice, 143–4; audiences
with, 144–5; calling M to
Palace, 143; nail-biting, 143;
planning present for M, 132;
staff, 157; working
relationship with M, 92,
144–5
elocution, 42
Emu, 160
Everage, Dame Edna, 6
Evert, Christopher, 84

Faith in the City, 162
Falklands War, 46, 127–8, 137,
150–2
Farnborough, 87–8
female impersonators, 6
Festival of Britain, 79
Financial Times, 2
Finchley, 65, 88, 91–8
Fish, Michael, 160
Fitzroy Nuffield Hospital, 152
Flood Street: move from, 3
Fonda, Jane, 94
Foot, Michael, 84, 92–3, 153–5
Forsyth, Bruce, 8
France: British claims, 71
Francis, Dick, 160

Fraser, Hugh, 136
French: illogicality of, 26
frugality: of father, 30; of M, 3,
   17, 37–8, 73, 111, 112–13; of
   mother, 20–1, 31, 82
furniture: tips on buying,
   112

Gaitskell, Hugh, 93
Galtieri, General, 150–1
Gandhi, Mrs Indira, 170
Gatting, Mike, 159
GCHQ (Government
   Communications
   Headquarters), 156–7
General Belgrano, 151
General Election: 1935, 29–30;
   1945, 50, 53; 1950, 64–5;
   1959, 89; 1964, 110; 1970,
   117; 1971, 129; 1979, 139–40;
   1983, 155, 156; 1987, 166
Gilmour, Ian, 93
Gorbachev, Mikhael, 160–1
Gorbachev, Raisa, 161
Gowrie, Lord, 50
grammar schools, 119
Grant, Russell, 160
Grantham: community, 9–10;
   North Parade: flat, 9; shop,
   12, 136
Grenada, 166
Grenfell, Joyce, 94
Gummer, John Selwyn, 4, 108,
   162
Hart, Dame Judith, 94
Healey, Denis, 92–3, 133, 160
Heath, Edward, 2, 92; attitude
   to women, 125; as bachelor,
   125, 126; causing crisis, 127;
   getting rid of, 167; ineptitude,
   115, 116–18; lacking in
   loyalty, 126; in leadership
   battle, 136; losing grip on
   reality, 125, 131, 136;
   mismanagement, 129, 133;
   obsession with boating, 126;
   resignation, 137; strange

ideas, 123–5, 127
Heseltine, Michael, 3, 15, 164
Hitler, Adolf, 30
hoarding, 136–7
Home of the Hirsel, Lord (Alec
   Douglas-Home), 109, 137
home ownership, 21, 131–2
hooligans, 149
House of Commons:
   hand-shaking not allowed,
   98; majesty of, 91; virus
   outbreak, 2
household tips, 111–14
housekeeping: likened to job of
   Prime Minister, 1
housing: policies on, 131
Housing Acts, 132
Howe, Sir Geoffrey, 1, 123,
   151, 156
Howe, Mrs, 3
hula-hoops, 76
Hull, Rod, 160
humour: amusing postman,
   13–14; startling children,
   18–19
Huntingdon Tower Road
   Elementary School, 14–18
Hurd, Douglas, 93

ice-cream: work on, 61–2
Immigration Bill, 144
inner cities: policy on, 162;
   problems, 145
Ireland, 165–6
Italians: governments, 169

Jenkins, David, 162
Jenkins, Roy, 92–3
Joan of Arc, 54
jokes: amusing postman,
   13–14; improving, 18–19;
   making up, 19; startling
   children, 18–19
Joseph, Keith, 133–5
journalists: opinion of, 97

Keeler, Christine, 108–9

Kesteven and Grantham Girls' School, 22–5
KGB: agents of, 158–9; suspected agents, 159–60
Kinnock, Glenys, 166

Labour Party: coalition with Liberals, 129; collapse of Government, 133; disappearance, 167; leader, 93; manifesto, 5; in power, 50, 53, 58, 87, 110, 130; reaction to Falklands War, 152; support for strikers, 96; value of, 167
Ladybird, Professor, 99–100
landlady: devotion to M, 55; sorrow at losing M, 61
Laski, Dr, 58
Lawson, Mrs, 3
Lawson, Nigel, 12, 62, 93, 100, 112, 124, 159
Levin, Bernard, 159
Liberal Party, 93–4, 129, 148
Libya, 40, 166
Liverpool: no need to live in, 155
Llandudno: Party Conference, 59
Lloyd, Joan, 84
Lloyd, Selwyn, 92–3, 98
Longford, Francis Pakenham, Lord, 51–2
Lyons & Co., J., 61–2

Macgregor, Ian, 163
Maclaine, Shirley, 6
Macmillan, Harold, 92–3, 100, 109
maiden speeches, 97–8
mathematics: importance of, 15–16
Maudling, Reginald, 125
Members of Parliament: different from actors, 87; liking for American actresses, 6; living in constituency, 61;

questioning PM, 5; salaries, 58, 73–4; unmarried, 125–6
Methodists: privileges for, 95, 163
MI5: allegations about, 158; disillusionment with, 159; list of suspects, 159–60
Michael of Kent, Princess, 159
milk: free milk abolished, 121–3; symbolism of, 25
milk bottle: incident of, 11
Millar, Ronnie, 145–6
miners' strike, 127–9
monetarism, 146–7
money: collecting in sofa, 112
Moore, Sir Philip, 143
Muir, Frank, 159
Murdoch, Rupert, 66, 96–7, 159
Muzorewa, Bishop, 147–8

nail-biting: cures for, 143
Nallon, Steve, 159
National Health Service, 9–10; help for, 152
National Union of Miners, 127
Neave, Airey, 138
newspapers: readable bits, 2, 57
Nicholson, Mavis, 159
Norden, Denis, 159
Norman (postman), 13–14
North, Colonel, 148
Northern Ireland: under-achievers going to, 115; useful role, 165
Northern Ireland Office, 165
NUJ, 84

Open University, 120
Operation Herod, 134
Opposition: importance of, 167
Owen, David, 156
Oxfam, 13
Oxford University, 37–53; Conservative Association, 49–52, 53–4; entrance to, 30–1; men at, 38–9, 46; present state of, 37

Pakenham, Frank, 51–2
Parkinson, Cecil, 109–10
Parliament: televising, 79;
  women in, 94
patents, 75–7
Patten, John, 93
pensioners: advice to, 101–2,
  136; not economical to live
  in sin, 111
Peruvian peace plan, 151
Peterson, Oscar, 159
pillars of community, 10
Pitt, William, the Elder, 170–1
Pitt, William, the Younger, 171
police force: management
  buyout, 164; wages, 129
politicians, *see* Members of
  Parliament
Potter, Mrs, 36
Powell, Enoch, 57, 115–16,
  159
Pre-Retirement Choice, 136
press: British, 84
Prevention of Terrorism Act,
  165
Prime Minister: job likened to
  housekeeping, 1
Prime Minister's Question
  Time, 5
Prior, Jim, 65
prisoners: importance of study
  for, 120
Private Member's Bill, 95–8
privatisation, 163–4
Profumo, John, 108–9
public spending: cuts in,
  119–22

Queen Charlotte's Hospital, 80

radio, 2, 21
Rainbow, 7
Reagan, ex-President Ronald,
  169; as actor, 22, 80; against
  Libya, 40; interest in politics,
  87; military insights, 166;
  relationship with M, 148–9

Redgrave, Vanessa, 94
Redhead, Brian, 159
revenue law, 77–9
rheumatism: *Daily Mirror*
  responsible for, 65
Rhodesia, 147–8
Ridley, Nicholas, 113
Roberts, Alfred (father):
  bringing home dead
  animals, 114; business
  with ship's captain, 59; civic
  duties with widow, 20;
  collecting souvenirs of
  Commons, 92; coping with
  fire-damaged stock, 149;
  disapproval of BBC, 21;
  disapproval of laughter, 18;
  education, 28–9; explaining
  political situation, 30;
  family, 9; housing project,
  72; hunting single-handed
  for air-raid survivors, 45–6;
  influence on M's education,
  28; interest in revenue law,
  77–8; as lay preacher, 10, 20;
  lessons learnt from, 31; loan
  from, 55; married
  happiness, 12; meeting
  Denis, 68–9; obsession for
  collecting, 44–5; pet name, 9;
  position in community, 10,
  11, 19–20; proposals for
  Private Member's Bill,
  95–6; readings by, 21;
  remarriage, 111;
  sacrifices for M's education,
  22–3, 31;
  self-improvement, 44; suing
  customers, 21–2; support
  for M, 59; thoughtfulness,
  43; thriftiness, 30; unable to
  campaign for M, 88; views
  on currency reform, 15;
  views on rates, 168; wartime
  service for community, 44–5;
  weakness for cowboy films,
  22

Roberts, Beatrice (mother):
birthday treat, 21; death,
111; extravagance, 111;
lessons learnt from, 31;
married happiness, 12;
message in letter, 43; sacrifices
for M's education, 22–3, 31;
skill as needlewoman, 20,
70; thriftiness, 20–1, 31, 82;
words of wisdom, 12
Roberts, Cissie (stepmother),
111
Roberts, Ebenezer
(grandfather), 9
Roberts, Muriel (sister), 9, 22,
100, 101; correspondence
with, 43; leaving home,
43–4; legacy from mother,
111; marriage, 58; sacrifices
for M, 23, 31
Robson, Bobby, 160
role-playing exercise: practised
in Cabinet, 146
Rotary Club, 30
Runcie, Robert, 51
Rupert, Uncle, 45
Russians: selling secrets to, 157

Saatchi brothers, 166–7
St James's Park: flowers from, 1
Saint-Laurent, Yves, 160
SAS: experience, 165; role in
Falklands War, 137
Savoy, 85
Scargill, Arthur, 127, 165
secrets: not many worth
selling, 157
self-discipline, 10–11
Sellafield, 148
Selsdon Park, 116
Sheffield, 152
shopping: pleasures of, 4
Sim, Alistair, 160
Sir Galahad, 152
SLD, 148
sleep: best times for, 1–2;
legislation needed on, 63

small businesses: creating, 147
smiling: importance of, 64
Socialists, see Labour Party
sofa: use as money box, 111–12
Somerville College, 37–53;
contemporaries at, 41–2;
principal, 53
Spycatcher affair, 158–9
Stansgate, Viscount, see Benn,
Anthony Wedgwood
Star Wars, 148
State Opening of Parliament, 4
Stevas, Norman St John, 126,
139
Stonehouse, John, 98
Sunday: thrill of, 20
Sunday trading, 95–6
Swan Court, Chelsea, 86
Swinging Sixties, 115

taxation system, 77–9
Tebbit, Norman, 153
television, 6–7, 79
Thatcher, Carol (daughter):
birth, 80–1; career, 170;
childhood, 83; in company,
83; journalism, 83–4; literary
talent, 84–5; naming, 82–3;
reasons for not marrying
Prince Charles, 149–50;
studies, 83; wearing
mother's shoes, 17
Thatcher, Denis Wilberforce:
board appointments, 111;
breakfast, 2; business efforts,
66; business trips to Las
Vegas, 85; campaigning for
M, 88–9; choice of name for
son, 82; choosing clothes for,
112; clothes sense, 6;
compared to chemistry lab,
27; compared to dog, 155;
compared to Murdoch, 66;
doing business with
Gorbachav, 160; as
employer, 118; in favour of
three-day week, 127; first

marriage, 67; first meeting
with M, 65–7; generosity,
75, 150; giving financial
advice, 135; help with tax
legislation, 99; honeymoon,
70–1; inability to
concentrate, 99; influence on
M, 65; inspiration from, 132;
loan from, 75; marriage to
M, 69–70; meeting M's
father, 68–9; missing big
moments, 81, 98, 102, 111;
pointing out misuse of
coins, 125; practicing
putting, 3; problem climbing
stairs, 3; proposal for Private
Member's Bill, 96; proposing
to M, 69; reasons for divorce,
67–8; as rugby referee, 78;
self-sacrifice, 75; sense of
humour, 66–7, 81; TV
favourites, 79; wartime
bravery, 67; wartime
experiences, 71; wedding
present suggestion for Prince
Charles, 150
Thatcher, Margaret Hilda (née
Roberts): achievements, 8, 73,
147, 169; admitting mistakes,
140; advising Queen, 143–4;
appearance, 54–5;
appointment to Ministry of
Pensions, 101; appreciating
value of scrimping and
saving, 23; ARP warden, 41;
at University, 30–1, 36,
37–53; attraction for Earl's
son, 46–9; avoiding men at
Oxford, 39; as baby, 135;
becomes leader of Party,
137; becomes MP, 89, 91–8;
becomes Prime Minister,
140; belief in share
ownership, 66; birth, 9; birth
of children, 80–1; brightness
of smile, 64; bust of, 37;
catch phrases, 147; cheated of

honorary doctorate, 37;
childhood, 9–36, 113–14;
choosing bishops, 162–3;
choosing subjects to study,
25–7; colleagues' farewell
to, 60–1; colleagues' pet
names for, 56; concern for
unemployed, 4–5; conflict of
duties, 129; considering
politics as career, 58–9;
cooking hints, 113–14; daily
routine at Oxford, 39; daily
routine as girl, 12–13, 14,
19–22; daily routine as PM,
1–8; as Defender of the
Faith, 162–3; degree, 54;
Denis's prosposal to, 69;
disadvantages of, 103, 108;
disapproval of female
impersonators, 6;
disapproval of unmarried
MPs, 125–6; dismissing
Cabinet members, 103;
draft speech to Party
Conference, 101–2;
education, 14–18, 22–8;
effect on men, 58; election
campaign, 62–5; elocution,
42; entering politics, 53–4,
60; entertaining: first
attempt, 48; European
leanings, 26–7; family life,
110–11; favourite song, 2;
first meeting with Denis,
65–7; first taste of politics,
29–30; forced to give up
being ordinary housewife,
140–1; functions attended, 6,
7; highbrow tastes, 7;
hoarding, 136–7;
honeymoon, 70–1; in hospital
with hand, 153; household
tips, 111–14; as human
being, 8; incapable of bearing
grudges, 126; introducing
Private Member's Bill, 95–8;
kissed by Whitelaw, 138;

Thatcher, Margaret Hilda – *cont.*
knowing how to talk to
people, 133; knowledge of
Latin, 57; leadership at
school, 24; learning
importance of hard work,
11–12; learning Latin, 27–8;
lessons learnt from parents,
31; love of canvassing, 62–5;
love of chemistry, 27; love of
Sunday, 20; love of westerns,
22; loyalty, 55; maiden
speech, 97–8; making
home, 3; marriage, 69–70;
milk monitor, 25; Minister
of Education, 117–23; in
Ministry of Environment,
131; as mother, 83; naming
twins, 82–3; newspaper
reading, 2, 57; opinion of
journalists, 97; outings at
child, 21–2; poem written
by, 81–2; popularity, 56;
president of Oxford
University Conservative
Association, 49–52; Prime
Minister, 102–3, 108;
pupillage as barrister, 74;
reading for Bar, 71–2, 74;
receptions, 6; relationship
with Reagan, 148–9;
relaxation, 5; responsibilities
at school, 17; school report,
36; scientific discoveries, 56;
secret ambition, 27; seeing
grandson as heir, 170–1;
selection as candidate,
59–60; self-discipline, 11;
sense of humour, 13–14,
18–19, 108; singing
performance, 40–1; sixth
sense, 122–3; sleep
requirements, 1–2, 63;
socialising, 49–50; sport at
school, 24; stamina, 170;
tasks for next 20 years, 171;
taste in dress, 54–5, 80; taste
in literature, 8, 25; taste in
make-up, 55; taste in music,
27; tea-drinking habits, 145;
television watched, 6–7;
thriftiness, 3, 17, 37–8, 73,
111, 112–13; tidiness, 1, 92;
time spent in House, 5;
timeless elegance, 80;
toothache, 167; travels, 4;
varicose veins operation,
152; vocation for public
service, 19–20; as wife, 74, 75,
78; working in American
airforce canteen, 40;
working at Lyons, 61–2;
working in chemical
company, 54, 55–7; working
on patents, 75–7; working
relationship with Queen,
144–5; working on revenue
law, 77–9
Thatcher, Mark (son): birth,
80–1; career, 170; childhood,
83; in company, 83; flair as
entrepreneur, 85; marriage,
85–6; naming, 82–3;
suggestions for M's opening
lines, 145
Thatcher, Michael (grandson),
170–1
Thatcherism, 146
Thomas à Becket, 160
Thorndike, Sybil, 86–7
Thorpe, Jeremy, 94
Toxteth, 149
trades unions: banning, 156–7;
electricians' strike, 41;
reform legistlation, 128
TUC: funds, 159
Two Ronnies, 7

unemployed: concern for, 4–5;
need to sue, 22; surprising
characteristics of, 4
unemployment: like
toothache, 167; Parliament's
contribution to reducing, 7

United Nations Charter, 166
Upper Heyford, 40

Valentine card, 148
Vaughan, Dame Janet, 53

Waiting for Godot, 87
Walden, Brian, 136
Wales, 151
Walker, Peter, 128
waste not, want not, *see*
  frugality
Waugh, Evelyn, 38
Wells, John, 149
Westland, 164–5
Whitelaw, William, 135,
  137–8; extract from

memoirs, 138–9
Wilde, Oscar, 133
Williams, Shirley, 21, 84, 121
Wilson, Harold, 116–17
Windscale, 148
women: in Parliament, 94;
  responsibilities, 94
Wright, Peter, 158–9

Yeovil, 164–5
Yes, Minister, 7
Yom Kippur War, 126
Young Conservative
  Conference, 137–8
YTS scheme, 73

Zimbabwe, 148